GORÉE'S UNWAVERING SONGS

Gorée's Unwavering Songs

Poetry

FEMI OJO-ADE

AMVPS

AMVPS

Published by

AMV Publishing

P.O. Box 661
Princeton, NJ 08542-0661
Tel: 609-2270220
emails: publisher@amvpublishingservices.com &
customerservice@amvpublishingservices.com
worldwide web: amvpublishingservices.com

Gorée's Unwavering Songs
Copyright © 2017 Femi Ojo-Ade

First Published in Nigeria in 2014 by Amoge Publishers Ltd., Lagos
E-mail: omooba_adeyemi@yahoo.com; Tel: + 234 8037017475

All rights reserved. No part of this publication may be reproduced, stored in a retrieval system, or transmitted in any form or by any means, electronic, mechanical, photocopying, recording or otherwise without the written permission of the publisher.

Cover Design: Dapo Ojo-Ade
Book Design: Ify Anyanwu

Library of Congress Control Number: 2016919796

ISBN: 9780989491785

For
Madiba, Malcolm, and Martin, and in memory of
Frederick Ivor Case, my teacher-mentor-brother

untitled   126
Congo-Kinshasa *(for Patrice Lumumba)*   127
memory and testimony *(for Fred Case, R.I.P)*   138

one   141
Glossary   143

TABLE OF CONTENTS

Acknowledgements ix
an invitation x
Preface xi

Gorée   1
being black *(for Frantz Fanon)*   14
faces and places *(for Afro-Brazil)*   18
a death in the family   20
poets and poetry *(for Aimé Césaire)*   22
my people, they just don't know *(for Ayi Kwei Armah)*   29
amnesia   36
poverty   38
beauty   40
paradox *(for Ngugi and Njeeri)*   43
obamaphobia   47
a fall from grace   51
religion   53
north and south   55
Bolt *(for Usain Bolt)*   57
one day in America   59
Africa, my Africa   62
civilisation   67
thanksgiving   68
Haiti   74
all about us and them   85
a national incident *(for victims of bomb attack)*   86
living while black   89
politics   94
ode to Africa's dinosaurs   99
love and pain   103
one life fulfilled *(for Nelson Mandela, Robben Island Prisoner #46664)*   106
God save us   120
terror   122

ACKNOWLEDGEMENTS

I express my gratitude to:

family and friends for constant support outstripping the boundaries of the enticing and enslaving greenback; Israel, Puerto-Rican brother and colleague, and fellow poet negotiating the chains and shackles of the ever baffling spider's web of our experience in the African Diaspora; Ropo, African brother and colleague, for being there to bring clarity to confused concepts, and Africans the world over, for their resilience and strength to survive in conditions euphemistically described as horrible.

an invitation

come, come,
flee from the fangs of their civilisation
the wonderland of wealth and cheap comfort and confused culture
free your mesmerised mind from the mirage of democracy
the freedom to have your brain drained
to shed your soul for the shadow of the other.

Africa's waiting... and wondering
about you.

PREFACE

This poetry collection has taken several years of reflection on lived and observed black experience in Africa — particularly, Nigeria and South Africa — and the Diaspora, precisely the United States of America, Brazil, and the West Indies. The reflection was often overtaken and outstripped by silence because, one must admit, being black in today's so-called global village is far from being a lark. With the identity comes a whole mixed bag of negativities, a plethora of stigmas imposed by the civilised (in reality, the word connotes its opposite, savage, given their acts of barbarity against their victims) upon us for being black. The trauma is so overwhelming that one is forced into silence; for, what can one do after making futile efforts to ameliorate Blacks' position of disenfranchisement and powerlessness and dehumanisation? Who will read your writing? Who cares? And your people, in particular, do they read? Are they interested? Do they have the means? Such questions could easily kill the will and make a normally effervescent brain comatose. They could make one lose one's senses, become alienated like a hermit living on the verge with no hope for any return to normalcy. Normalcy itself, one must never forget, is not a better option; for, it is fraught with its heavy dose of acceptance of the impunity of the oppressors in their acts of bold-faced victimisation. You write and continue to write with the hope for change gradually diminishing until hope becomes hopelessness.

Now, when silence becomes an unbearable burden of uselessness — thank goodness for the embers of commitment refusing to die — the soul returns to life and the desire to try again overcomes the nothingness of silence. That is what this new collection represents for me. The poems represent a new belief, a new faith, in the themes and thrust of poetry, with what the great poet from Martinique, Aimé Césaire, calls the poem's less becoming more. In essence, this poet believes in the possibility of revolution and these poems would hopefully be read as a modest contribution to that process whereby the people, my people, would awaken from their slumber, stand up for their rights, fight for their freedom, and claim the power that belongs to them.

Poetry is concise and precise, focused upon essentials, in Africa's case, the necessity for freedom and change and re-awakening from centuries of slumber induced by invaders from the north with the later assistance of internal colonisers consciously, and sometimes unconsciously, colluding in the destruction or devaluation of our culture. From the onset, our poetry has remained different from the form-driven European tradition where rhyme would stand in competition with reason and where the message would often have secondary consideration in importance. For us, message matters; for, without a doubt, the people, engaged in the struggle for survival in complex conditions and under corrosive circumstances, need to have vital information as regards their existential dilemma. If message matters, that does not mean that form is of no importance. After all, beauty is a combination of material and moral components. Aesthetics and ethics come together to awaken the reader from his slumber. Poetry thus constitutes food for thought and, similar to other art-forms, it is provocative and people-centred.

The choice of free verse is expressive of a revolutionary stand on the part of the poet. Rejection of restriction. Proclamation of rights. Declaration of freedom. Such are the driving forces of the poetic enterprise. In short, by breaking the aesthetic bonds, the poet is declaring his freedom and making a choice to break all forms of shackles impeding his people's progress in a world ironically caught in the web of neocolonialism even as it is being hailed for a new era of freedom and equality and human rights. In this collection, the rules of the game are deliberately contravened. The capital letter is often eschewed for the lower case. The lines run on with no particular formal construct. Rhymes exist, but not quite often. The driving force for the form here is freedom, a revolutionary standpoint emphasising the poet's determination to reject any imposition. Revolution entails both rejection and re-affirmation: while the poet distances himself from the European tradition, he is also aware of the necessity to assert his art's Africanness; hence, capital letters are used for persons and places. People, human beings, will be engaged in revolution which will take place in human habitats.

The overarching objective is to use the poetic word and voice as the means of true liberation, as facilitator of freedom, as projection of the people's deepest desires that, under prevailing conditions and circumstances, have been held in bondage. The titles of the poems underscore these points.

As stated earlier, Africa and the Diaspora are brought together as a matter of course: the bridges broken by the enslavers have to be re-built; the cultural, social, and human ties truncated by an experience unmatched by any other in its brutality and barbarity have to be revived. In this poet's opinion, continuities, collaboration and complementarity have to replace contradiction, conflict and condemnation. Without Africa, the Diaspora would be but a floating mass without roots. Without the Diaspora, Africa would be an isolated mass in the jungle of the civilisers' nightmares. Some of the poems in this collection show clearly the bonds between those that were forced out of the original motherland and those left behind. Besides, as the migrant bug continues to bite continentals desperate to escape from the gulag of their homelands for the supposed paradise of Euro-America, they come together with their cousins, citizens of the Diaspora new homes, to revise and update the definition of identities. In the long run, both the continental and the diasporic share an identity from which they would benefit immensely, if they are committed to their culture and civilisation. Of course, the civilisers, fully aware of the potential of such African-American engagement, are busy discouraging it by encouraging the age-old notion of the dichotomy between African savagery and American civilisation. As with everything else, it is left to us to make or break our destiny.

It is noteworthy that critics generally pay particular attention to writers' generations in discussing and dissecting their works. Writers are supposed to address issues particular and peculiar to their generations. To our mind, such a position serves a negative purpose for Africa. Generation gap, one daresay, is a concept of division and diversion. It is irrelevant and inadequate in the African context where struggle for change is a continuum, where our lived experiences are a flowing river of constant and complex ebb and tide, from colonialism to neocolonialism. Freedom has been the ruse called Independence. Our leaders have become the new masters evolving from their tutelage under the European invaders into internal colonisers that have to be dislodged from the mountain-top mansions similar to those occupied by the departed commandants.

The concept of generations would be relevant in other climes where history is a date, fixed by the specificity of an act, such as a law signed, sealed and delivered. Thus, the United States civil rights law of 1964 marked the end of black revolutionary era, the resolution of racism as a cancer cornered and conquered forever. The law is finality, and the problem is eradicated once and for all. Supposedly, one must insist, however; for, rather than eradicating the problem, the law has only given Americans reason to be complacent, to bask in the aura of a paradise shallow and shady, allowing and encouraging people to engage in amnesia, and to use hypocrisy to hide hate. Indeed, in many cases, hate now rears its ugly head in the open, with pride, with pomposity, as it claims the supremacy of White over all else. Under the circumstances, one is not surprised that many young Blacks are ignorant and unaware of the civil rights struggle: they are made to believe that the law has taken care of "the black problem" and, therefore, it is time to move on. Moving on means forgetting history, forgetting one's heritage, forgetting one's present dilemma, and selling one's soul for the right of place in "free" society where one would blend as a faceless shadow without substance.

What we are proposing here is an all-generation, African concept of culture and struggle. It is the only appropriate way of capturing the realities of our experience of dehumanisation that cuts across ages and communities even as the masters of the modern plantation keep trying to date and dictate the details of that experience. In theory, our countries have evolved from colonies to nations through independence that brought them to the nirvana of Freedom. On the contrary, Truth tells us that not much has changed from past to present. Writers, poets, from all generations, if they are honest and committed, would hardly have any divergent views of our experience. Our struggle, engaging the minds and bodies of one and all, needs to be a matter of communality, not individuality. We must insist upon responsibilities (whole group), not rights (self, encouraging selfishness). Wasted, washed out, wasteful, whatever generation, we are all caught in the continually complex and confused long night in the darkness of oppression and misery from which, together, we all have to struggle to emerge into the light of freedom and human dignity.

We repeat: rhyme is not a fundamental aspect of this poetry collection. For one thing, rhyme is a rarity in our lives, lives marked by consequences of times past still impacting the present in various negative ways. Basic reason tells us that we must deal with realities so as to overcome, to vanquish all those people and places standing in the way of our liberation and progress. So, these poems are immersed in the rhythm of reason, of rights, of revolution, indeed, in the struggle for survival and revival.

Gorée

here at last!
after many travels both vertical and horizontal
now I'm at the Door of No Return
where my ancestors were stripped of their humanity
in preparation for the journey to living death in the white man's new world
where dreams were slaughtered by nightmares in the darkness of his so-called civilisation.

I'm home at last
to re-live that long season of short sessions of shattering shots of dehumanisation
here to imagine how the human cargo was readied for transportation away forever
yet I wonder about my imagination
imagination is vicarious experience is a sham
imagination helps us to hide behind the security of time and place
imagination is not experience is not the present is only a view of the past from protected present
imagination is cozily conceived as past history to be dusted up and dissected in the comfort of your sitting-room among friends sipping wine
imagination is inadequate but inevitable and viable if we bring the spirit of honesty and desire for truth
imagination may owe its authenticity to identity
its value may be adduced to the distinction between slave and enslaver
between blood descendants of the beast owning and

controlling the House of Slaves in Gorée
and those whose forebears were swallowed into the belly of the beast
it's all in the body language of visitors to the historic island.

Gorée is an island in the sun
an impressive paradise from a distance
a stone's throw from the shores of mainland Dakar with its stench and suffering masses
the waters between mainland and island are sky blue and serene
with swimmers skillfully gliding with the surf
and waves weaving wondrous patterns along the surface
big boats including colonial-era and neo-slavery ships are anchored off the coast
while a few bearing export from Senegal are plodding along in a slow departure toward western destinations
on the sea endless enticing strange and solemn
on this same sea went ships with human cargo in their horrible holds
ships aptly named Destiny-Hope-Freedom-Joy
they glided along majestically serving as means of dastardly machinations and manipulations
on the sea of no return but also of inevitable return.

my American students and I make the crossing from Dakar in a chaloupe loaded with modern travellers
we are a global village of various colours between black and white
we are friends and family and strangers and associates all visiting Gorée for many goals
tourists and researchers and seekers of solace in these trying times and curious visitors to the shrine of calumny in these times of human triumph over evil

Femi Ojo-Ade

we are all together in this moment of excitement
each with a right of presence and personal purpose.

my students and I are on an academic mission — in theory
in truth, it's more a power play of plenty over poverty
it's a form of tourism sweetened by the palatable sauce of education
an experience that bolsters careers with its international and cultural image
and makes the Gorée graduate an expert on everything African.

my students are in their element with other tourists
appropriately dressed for carnival
armed with i-phones and i-pads and other instant gratification-resolution gadgets
and ready to record for their posterity waiting at home every second of the wonderful occasion
they all rejoice with their outsiders' cheeky peep into the tortured world of the oppressed and dispossessed
they are sending endless phone texts and selfies
they pay more attention to mementos and less to memory.

since Gorée does not tell their story
they show curiosity but not consciousness
they cannot get into the skins of slaves
because their forebears were not slaves but masters of slaves and history
they are quick to pose with statues and other symbols
erected in honor of Boufflers and other governors of Gorée
all heroes of doom
they are not attracted to graffiti messages such as this scribbled by a slave:
To you that may read this story, do not end it with

forgetfulness. Leave restored in your memory this cry that is mine and that of other men and listen to your heart.
they climb onto the iconic canon of the famed film *Guns of Navarone*
with no recognition of its role in protecting changing ownership of the island and prosecuting the war of nationalistic hegemony with Africa as pawn and property of the civilised brothers
they show more interest for the island's fat and frightful cats and less in the street children begging for bread.

our guide is a strapping young man full of vibrancy
enthused and well versed in the history of the trade and the transition and transformation of Africans to Americans
he is not shy to show off his skills at thematic control and rhythmic undulation and modulation
he relishes the process of embellishing and diminishing details of a drama determining the destiny of his and my race
performance seems to be the prime project
as the aspiring griot's preening and prancing and punching the air with transparent pride
exaggeration or truth?
no matter.

the height of excitement is attained at the House of Slaves
where octogenarian Director Boubacar Joseph Ndiaye holds sway
on a stage fit for royalty
he reminds of our young guide and the comparison heightens the old man's superiority
he too is a griot but in the vein of a virtuoso mixing the spontaneous free-flowing rhythm of jazz with the well-defined calibrated coda of classical chant
his mellifluous voice at once brings solemnity to a raw tragic

tale and attracts one's attention to the horror of holes called
rooms where the slaves were stashed while awaiting the final
passage
his baritone complemented by well inserted silence makes
one think of the mystique and mystery of negro spirituals
his message is magically meaningful as manifested in the
face of an ebony beauty with intricate braids simultaneously
shedding silent tears and smiling a sweet smile
he stands upright exuding pride and confidence like the
griots of yore
he cuts the figure of perennial paternal presence as protector
of the people's treasure
he lends authenticity depth dignity to a profession lately
dumped into the depths of triviality by hawkers and hustlers
of money and material
he raises the bar of the enslavers' beastly behavior
he increases the threshold of the slaves' suffering and
survival and strength
to levels fit for the annals of legendary kingdoms of empires
razed by northern colonisers
he reels off facts and figures to the delight and dismay of the
gawking crowd of seekers of pleasure and others of solace
and emotional appeasement
we enter the transit rooms for specific categories of the
captured human cargo
categories marked by deep racist bias and irreducible desire
for debasement of the human soul
"temporarily inapt-recalcitrant-men-women-children-
girls" were stored like sardines in cells not even suitable for
animals
and we see chains and balls and other gadgets of torture to
tame and turn humans into slaves
and we learn that the first slave house in Gorée is now a
presbyterian church

and we read that the slaves *went with their eyes fixed upon
the infinite of suffering.*

the house of slaves has an exhibition room with quotations
on boards
such as the claim that all human societies have engaged in
slavery
with the African example being *a form of punishment and
loss of freedom.*
no wonder the world's master manipulators have succeeded
in diminishing the unique tragedy of our enslavement by
calling slavery any form of impediment to freedom
as if a slap on the face were as serious as horse-whipping on
the bare buttocks dangling from a tree
as if exploiting a poor teenager as house help were
tantamount to life on a plantation
as if recruiting willing migrants for Euro-American farms
and factories were comparable to the pogrom visited upon
our ancestors.

as we follow the director's silent footsteps
down the dark and dinghy alley leading to the dreaded door
of the final deportation
we have the feeling of descending the dungeon toward death
we feel the harrowing loss of all things human
we sense the shedding of the soul's essence
and the replacement of freedom by total control and
coercion
the beginning of the end, was it?

the saga on the sea of the middle passage tells the tale of
courage on boats manned by civilised beasts
the deported refused to accept their fate as final

they refused to accept the living death of forced deracination
and exile
they refused to succumb to the humiliation of the enslaving
captain and his dastardly crew
they willingly embraced the depths by a sudden plunge
while others, just as revolted in rejecting any other place but
home,
were thrown overboard on boats symbolically named
Freedom and Friendship
murder and suicide underscored revolution and resilience
and resistance
that would become the driving force of slave communities in
the Americas
the spirit of resistance and the soul of rebellion gave birth to
maroon societies
that asserted their sovereignty in the face of the master plan
of colonisation and exploitation
based upon the cynical separation of families and ethnic
groups
from the initial haggling over slaves in the public square
to the policy on plantations programmed to please the
master's most outrageous caprices.

Africa's children did not die
they resisted
they survived through centuries of struggle
until freedom reigned
even as racism remains a die-hard reaction.

the road from past to present has been dotted with constant
criminality against Africanity
from slavery to KKK to Jim Crow to Civil Rights one
witnesses

various phases of the same concept of racism with black
condemned to the bottom
hounded by hooded human dogs and hung by a rope to a
tree in civilised America
encouraged to hang on to the dead dream of owning forty
acres and a mule
legally segregated to hell-holes of material misery by official
laws of white supremacy
and put out to pasture in penitentiaries where black is a
constant majority.

America — the United States of — is unique in the whole
wide world
as a federation of states succeeded in stealing the name and
identity of two continents
no wonder everyone is desirous of joining the dream train
no wonder many of Africa's children on the slavery train
were convinced to become American
slaves developed into citizens as the logical consequence of
afro-pessimism
and the reality of today's plethora of dilemmas
thus proving the necessity and relevance of Gorée.

other Americas have ceded Eurocentric crusade to the
United States
while cementing their Latinity in the cemetery of Africanity
images of Africa were overwhelmed by a new mix of culture
and colour
with black overshadowed by an off-white contraption
miscegenation has reigned supreme under cover of the
concept of nation.

all Americas meet at the crossroads of colours and cultures
where conflicts and contradictions are resolved and Africa is
confirmed

in her alien status in Euro-America
either by Americanisation or by Latinisation
Africans have been made pawns and prostitutes
in status subordinate and submissive and subhuman
Africans in America have been forcibly reborn and bred in a nation
proclaiming its principles of humanism but visibly living
according to the laws of barbarity
a society blessed with elements of greatness but obsessed
with excesses of smallness
and exhibiting a shocking manicheistic ethos
in which Africa's exiled children are conditioned and
confused by promises of the dream
of material wealth
of mental hardiness
of moral supremacy
they constitute a community held in civilised bondage
nay, caught in limbo between America and Africa
yet they have survived.

their ex-Africans are not *good negroes*
they are not servants of civilisation
they are in their large numbers conscious of the politics of power
while some thank the Lord for saving their forebears from savagery
most consistently consider themselves as children of Africa
while some see themselves as superior and supreme Americans
most see such supremacism as offshoot of endemic racism
most look across at Africa for continuity and cooperation
most look back at Africa for inspiration and aspiration
thus we return to Gorée.

Gorée was owned by Europe's major players of slavery and colonialism
Gorée was coveted by nazis
Gorée was symbol of a civilisation gone crazy
hunting down and capturing humans like animals
stripping them naked beyond the skin to their soul.

yet Gorée has not totally kept its lure and allure as symbol of something deep and essential
because of the materialism of modernity
authorities Senegalese and French seem to have taken for granted
the island's insularity as pointer to the inaccessibility of iniquities
as if the distance from Dakar were an eternity
and the sanctity of the island an absolute reality.

a question of images it is
with material-mind-matter
all infused with the paternalistic ideologies of the world's self-chosen messiahs
Gorée is separated from Dakar
yet it complements and continues Dakar
yet it is an offshoot of Dakar
even if history insists on separation
for purposes of history and hype and politics and power.

in truth, Gorée is another modern resort for adventurous tourists
eager to cavort and gambol on the sweet soft sands of exotic seashores
away from the hubbub and hubble-bubble of their insane societies.

and affirmation of connection and continuity
notwithstanding modernity's mesmerising machinations
as the masters feed upon a breakfast of bias
as they devour a lunch of lies
as they fancy a dinner of dastardly acts
in a programme of progressive retrogression
that makes it imperative for Africans
to return home
which they did to Liberia and Sierra-Leone and other spaces
specific or accidental
chosen by white and black America urging ex-slaves to
return to *their jungle*
or to embark on a return to *civilise the worst and dumbest*
left behind at the time of forced departure.

Gorée
is a necessity for millennial action of revolution
with the compelling experience of our ancestors acting as
springboard for pushing forward
the pulsating passion for true freedom
in a recalcitrant global village refusing to sanction our
humanity
rejecting our plea for equality
repeating sins of their forebears against our humanity.

we return to Gorée
not as tourists not as pleasure-seekers not as curiosity-mongers
but as Africa's children seeking the warmth and wisdom of
our forgotten mother
we come to reinvent ourselves with memory
we come to revive our hopes after centuries of hopelessness
couched in a false dream
we come to reinforce our for long latent conviction in the

Gorée is a popular film location
a commercial centre
where the passion for trade in goods has replaced
yet replicates the insane enthusiasm for the other tragic
Trade
street children peddling groundnuts and other products of meagre returns
vie for space with big-chested girls hardly beyond puberty
running to present their wares to goggle-eyed tourists
possibly with intentions beyond the banana baskets dangling on the girls' heads
cats and dogs compete for the attention of compassionate Europeans
fawning upon the animals in a manner reminiscent of their ancestors on plantations of yore.

a pop band attaining ascendancy on the competitive national music scene
is playing a night date on the Gorée square
the crowd's as boisterous as and beat-struck as the reputedly riotous revellers of the mainland
stars of stage and stadium arrive to perform a rite of passage similar to age-old pilgrimage
to ancestral shrines
one and all come to worship at the altar of suffering and reflection
become the focus of fun and loss of memory
here at Gorée, symbol of perfunctory reconciliation and rehabilitation of a race once
disgraced.

Gorée
notwithstanding the cankerworm of commodification
looms large as flashpoint of our new awakening

authenticity of our faith in the colour and culture black
we hereby pay homage to the chained and shackled that
walked through the door of no return
we honour the plantation population of centuries gone by
pioneers of resistance
they struggled for our survival
they died in body so that they and us may live in body and
soul.

we come to Gorée over and over again
not the microcosm of capitalistic madness called free trade
not the melting pot of merry-makers
not the point of regular return of seekers of the sun
Gorée
is the wake-up call for slumbering children of Africa
the door of discovery of facts of our sufferings past and
present in the hands of dealers of death
the portal to our paradise on earth to be constructed by our
free labour of love.

Gorée
tells us that the struggle is not over
that we must stop being gladiators in the masters' arena
stop being stooges
stop being servants
stop
    being
        slaves.

being black
(for Frantz Fanon)

different strokes for different souls
being black is
black like a day without bread
black like the devil come down from high hell.

black like the bright side of the sun
black like
being.

black like mother earth feeding her children with honey
black like night and its mysteries leading to the dawn of a
new day.

different strokes for different souls
black hero
symbol of success
bearer of the banner of bastardisation
black pandering to blanchitude
he knows nothing of negritude
he lives a life of lies
he sings the praise of paternalism protecting poverty with
impunity
and projecting their superiority and supremacy with alacrity
he smiles while his people are suffering
black skin colourless clueless soul
white-washed and brain-dead
black forever climbing the ladder to white heaven.

Femi Ojo-Ade

different strokes for different souls
another black hero
he protests against his people's poverty
he projects faith in the future of his motherland
he uplifts his people spiritually psychologically materially
culturally and eternally
he stands up symbolically
and never reluctantly.

while the white-washed brother
epitome of hybridity and duplicity
displays his usual propensity for compromise
with the master of the millennial plantation
making false promises to the population
the house negro product of lust and rape
or maybe of love and rapture
collusion his name is
confusion his blame is
as he forgets that material and money cannot will not
change the colour and conscience
black.

same strokes for all souls
black
sentenced to purgatory of poverty amidst plenty
committed to a lifetime term in the ghetto of dearth disease
and death
notwithstanding knowledge wealth acquired
by heroes aware of what is required
by the masters and mistresses of capitalism
where other ideologies such as socialism
are viewed with opprobrium
in the new millennium
of their global village.

different strokes for different souls
being black is
notwithstanding games of the global village
allowing for continuous pillage
of our senses and souls
the same old story of struggle
against the same old nemesis
it is
waging war against neo-imperialism
concretised in capitalism
it is
standing as one against masters old and new of exploitation
camouflaging as partners of cooperation
it is
engaging in the enterprise of re-invention
continental and diaspora together in a free-flowing motion
immersed in unity and honesty
in the footsteps of new leaders awash with integrity
and pride of purpose
and the commitment of
being
     black
it is
refusing to be an observer of anyone's reality
rejecting being an object of anyone's history
it is
saying NO to anyone making us hate our history and heritage
a resounding NO to anyone humiliating our heroes
it is
revealing the hypocrisy of their altruism
reviling the fatalism of afro-pessimism
sneering at the generosity of saviours and mentors
spitting at the paucity of intelligence of their collaborators

it is
being
    black
        because
it is
human.

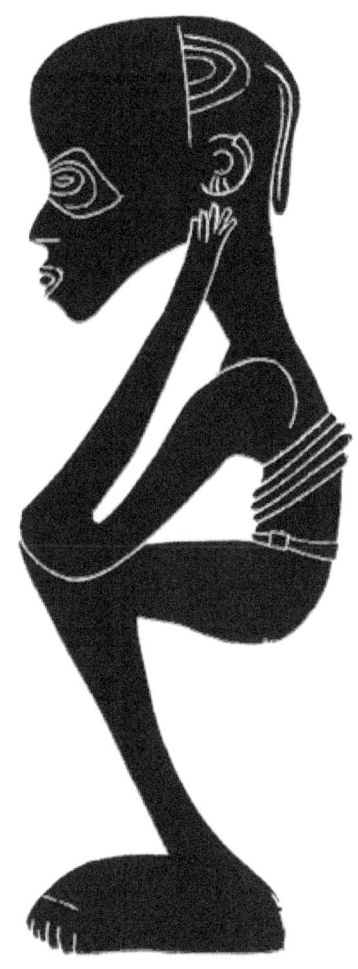

faces and places

(for Afro-Brazil)

the confusing yet exhilarating face of a cosmopolitan crowd
shades of the rainbow
how d'you pick out black?
black like Brasília
blue eyes
white collar
black like São Paulo
brown eyes
blue collar
black like Bahia
brown eyes
black colour
black at the bottom
they call it racial democracy
a choice of colour
with black at the bottom.

the confusing face of a cosmopolitan crowd
shades of white
no problem picking out black
like a dark dot in a sea of white
white as snow
white as pale
blonde hair blue eyes
still black at the bottom
in places named centres of their civilisation.

the confusing yet exhilarating face of a cosmopolitan crowd
how do you reach the soul from the surface?

how do you judge the heart from the face?
how do you fathom the depth of the place?
how do you know not to misplace
hope
in faces and places
so very confusing and sometimes exhilarating?

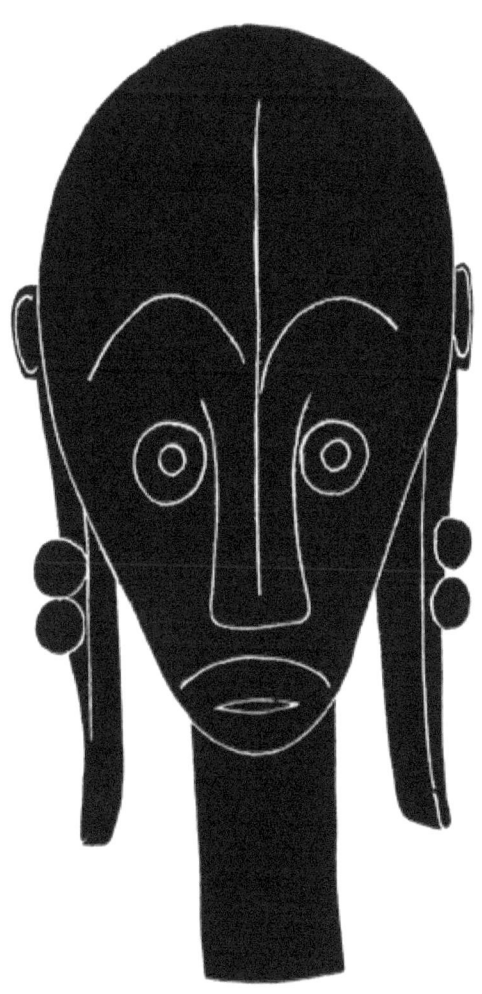

a death in the family

a death in the family
remember
when our light darkness came to dim
when our future yesterday became
when our happiness was into helplessness harried
when life became a worthless disphony of sad songs?

remember
when children suddenly lost their innocence
upon hearing news making no sense
recounted by messengers of death
even as they swore that all was well?

remember
when masked marauders proclaimed the joy of living
in coercion and collusion with philanthropists forever giving
the gift of oppression and repression
to those whose destiny they have mortgaged
for castles in their civilisation?

remember
when in the waking hours of a beautiful day
they brought her home cold but conscious
the body was bent but not broken
the eyes were a tell-tale of secrets never revealed
of betrayal and hate and contempt
where love supposedly reigned supreme?

remember

the children smiling at the sunshine before sobbing at the sight
of the body lying there undercover
like the tragedy of a shameful truth?

I remember
the pathos of a past for a while submerged
in a promising present soon supplanted
by a future irradiated with material success masking moral senility.

I remember
a motherless child making do with cow milk
and water from a mud-riddled well
a teenager at the beck and call of mean-spirited masters
an adult seeking salvation in the land of other masters
considered by all and sundry as civilised saviours
in the land where parenting is a pastime
for pimps and pastors
and fathers keep family with the penitentiary
and mothers marry drugs and death.
remember?

poets and poetry
(for Aimé Césaire)

a friend asks the poet:
*but why have you been so silent
why
have you been holding back on your legendary loquacious
tongue-lashing?
why
nothing on our dear nation's struggles in the face of myriad
issues of corruption and underdevelopment?*

the poet scratches and shakes his bald head with an
inscrutable smile etched on his aging face
what can he say that has not been said?
what can he describe that has not been described?
what can he condemn that has not been condemned?
by others before him and by him and others after him?
he has lived what some would call a happy life
of freedom of movement and material comfort and a
modicum of psychological stability
interpreted by the optimistic majority as the hallmark of
happiness.

it's all about whom and what and why and how
where history has had a sad lasting legacy often overlooked
by the liars of historiography
because they as globalist manipulators make us objects of
our lived experience even as
we strive to shake the shackles and flee the dungeon into the
daylight of subjectivity
it's all about us and them

and we have insisted on telling the tales of too many tragedies and too few triumphs
as we have too often blamed them and not us for sins of connivance and collusion
in our land of corruption imposed and self-imposed from home and abroad
by them and us both locked in a conundrum created by an engagement marked by inequalities and iniquities.

the silence of the poet may be adduced to a sense of shame for chronic crimes of senselessness
and greed and graft and prostitution of the very soul of a people blessed with plenty
and return to the past and a present without a future
in a place where one step forward is followed by a thousand backward
while the new leaders are proclaiming the extraordinary triumph of progress
and unparalleled development through their patriotic programmes.

the poet claims to be committed to his people
he wishes to be the voice of the voiceless
he submits to the view of the great Martinican Césaire that poetry is eruption and a means of
revelation and the essential word and a less transformed into a more and a
creation of a zone of incandescence where the flower of the self blooms
and that beautiful flower must be kept alive like an ulcer.

first there is beauty
beauty of self and spirit open to the four winds of a world of great possibilities

earth water air all elements of nature making for our existence and survival
beauty centred upon the dignity and drive of humanity to achieve and add
something tangible to the self and to the society
but beauty is not allowed to stand alone
in the complex and confused contact of selves feeding egos unrelenting and irredeemable in their
quest for supremacy
as they are determined to flush all opposition down the sewage of the newly brewing dross.

beauty of self encounters ugliness of society
as the poet endeavours to make beauty reign supreme
in a society where selfishness is a supreme cancer
the poet's power of the word helps the transformation of the less to the more
to the benefit of the community hopefully immune from the threatening claws of the voracious vultures
such is the hope of the zone of luminescence lighting up any darkness
destroying any devilish designs
bringing joy to the souls of one and all
breaking the chains of exploitation and building bridges of cooperation
as the flower of the self blooms into a bouquet of the community
and the poet vows to stand at the vanguard of the committed crowd
to make sure that the bonds of love and togetherness in struggle do not break
particularly because of a certain immediate reality hidden to the unwary and the careless.

the flower beautiful like the dawn of a new day
lithesome luscious
ideal idyllic
the flower is surrounded by thorns of transgressions and travails
the flower is caught in the web of an ulcer threatening to etiolate and eliminate it
with the poet serving as agent of consolation and consolidation
as creator and constructor and contributor not
as outsider and silent observer excommunicated in his own land
as initiated inserted injected into Africa's earth and beyond the ancestral continent
into a diaspora community captured in capitalism yet conscious of a continuous current
flowing back and forth across the seas in search of something special and essential
to the survival of our culture and civilisation.

the poet is tired of visiting and revisiting the frozen imagery of patriotic villainy and violence
and the otiose accretion of neocolonialism's imperialistic exploitation
but
the poet cannot afford to remain tired
a matter of chance or choice?
a question of submission or subversion?
the only viable choice is the word the rhythm and the rhyme
even where nothing rhymes
the word hard and harsh as the retribution against nationalist nincompoops and
soft and sweet as the lullaby welcoming to the world children of hope

and the rhythm of life and love
of duty and desire
of rights and responsibilities
it keeps stirring the people's souls into action
it keeps arousing defeated dreams into a new day of
determination and faith.

the poet is not tired
his poetry is a committed craft for popular consumption
with vistas of bliss and beauty in a blighted and bleak
landscape
from which millions are desperate to escape
his task is to dissuade his people from the short cut of escape
and alienation
his task is to encourage them to stay and struggle
because home is the source and centre of hope for happiness
because the criminals killing hope and happiness deserve to
be defeated
to be dragged in the mud of their dastardliness
to be disgraced and dislodged to the bottom of the pit where
they belong
because the people deserve a developed and peaceful land
where they and their children can thrive in decency.

the poet cannot be tired
yet he remains tired
because he cannot forget that his freedom of movement and
his life of comfort
are privileges out of reach of his poor people?
because he must be realistic and truthful to that beauty of
the soul that propels his word
because he lives in constant fear that he may one day lose his
mind.

such is the conflict the confusion the controversy of the word
brief in its beauty and convincing in its concision
yet inadequate and impossible in that very precise beauty
as the less negotiates the rocky road of transformation into
the more
the free flow of emotions gushing forth with gusto like the
black gold of the Niger delta
counters yet complements
the slowly sliding sentiments of a heavy heart seeping
through like blood from the body of a victim battered by
bandits.

the poet cannot despair
knowing as he does that he must descend from his
capitalistic heights
to share the neocolonial hell hole with his beleaguered
people
like a bird soaring in the skies majestic and magnificent
must perch on a tree and enjoy the company of other free
habitants of happy horizons
better like a stowaway compelled to abandon the housing
project of civilisation's ghetto
to return to his village hut surrounded by nature's beauty
and the potential for growth in a community of the
committed wretched of the earth.

the poet cannot demur
knowing that his contribution may seem minor but is major
because integrity is in short order
because accountability is a tall order
because corruption is in order
because those certain of their commitment cannot afford to
hesitate or hold back
they have to be firmly grounded with the people

like the *iroko* tree bastion of our age-old beliefs
backbone of our precious progressive culture
rooted in the depths of the earth
fatigue may set in and faith may flag
when time without change for the better takes its toll
nonetheless the spirit of the fighter must remain firm
the poet must remain symbol of struggle and survival
until the bell tolls for the end of man's existence
that does not negate the immortality of ideas expressed by
the transcendental word with timeless tenure and thrust.

my people, they just don't know
(for Ayi Kwei Armah)

let me introduce you masters potent and potential to the
people my people
faceless
nameless
hapless
harmless
hopeless
the ones you claim to love
the ones you lie to
the ones you lead to the precipice and abandon there
the ones you often lynch
democratically despotically
as dictators always do
the people my people
nobody
nothing
nowhere.

let me read for you from the book of gullibility
my people fall prey to the rent-a-crowd agenda of the power-
hungry cabal
they fill the vast space of political venues
they show sham support for no-policy propaganda
they get paid less than a pittance from loose change cornered
by their fanatical foremen lackeys of the leeches employing
their shameless services.

let me tell you about the comical theatre bankrolled by
those ready to rule at all costs over a people upon whom they
stomp and trample

my people are easy victims of the run-a-scam clan
they accept deceit and deprivation as their destiny
they look up to their victimisers as valorous visionaries and saviours
they pray assiduously for those emptying the country's coffers and playing big boys and girls in God's house.

let me share with you incontrovertible facts stranger than fiction
my people sing songs of praise for phantom projects
they praise God for candle-light electric power available all of one hour out of twenty-four
they applaud hilariously when the power holders claim to have made a quantum leap in national production even when there is visible evidence that the whole system is in its death-throes
they sigh with relief when the tenant on the symbolic rock announces another trillion greenbacks for repair of roads that continue to suck human blood as sacrifice for the nation's concocted unity.

let me read for you from the book of hunger and pain
my people can barely eat the semblance of a meal a day while dreaming of earning a dime a day
they toil until their backs are forever bent in a posture reminiscent of slaves on the plantation
they live in slum shacks with the only water running through their brick-laden cubicles
they fall sick with diseases diagnosed by quacks as endemic malaria and typhoid and borrow money to buy fake medicine that moves them faster and closer to their commoner cemetery.

let me tell you what you already know about my people
they have a pauper's passion for suffering

they are weird worshippers of wealth with the conviction that today's robbers will one day be replaced by other fortunate ones among whom the poor blessed by the Almighty may find themselves
they flock to the sites of newfound carnival where dancing dames and damsels dressed in uniforms and diminishing morals flaunt their natural endowments before the gaping and ogling eyes of lecherous admirers and dreaming commoners.

let me say a little more about my people
displeased
displaced
destabilised
disarmed
defeated
certain of their suffering in silence
afraid to speak to breathe to sneeze
for fear that someone would break their brittle bones
cut off their tongues
short-circuit their existence
in the dark of the night or in the dawn of despair
as they wait for the command of someone sitting and shitting on them.

my people just don't know
they are follow-follow fools
shadowless souls
shattered spirits
their dead dreams are drifting with the flotsam on the seas
leading to the savagery of foreign lands they call paradise
they are caged in limiting projects of poverty and powerlessness

they are happy and remain hopeful with laughter of
joylessness bursting through their darkest hour
their monochrome of a life is too clear for them to see in the
hands of monsters camouflaged as messiahs and saboteurs
as saviours and hustlers as heroes in the hustlers' heaven
called Nigeria.

my people just don't know
but they do know slowly but surely but slowly
everyone is tired
and how sufferness no go tire person?
they know that baba rigger-in-chief called president lies
when he says
we will offend God if we do things to bring pain to Nigerians
because criminals always hide behind God
my people are humble believers without power
so they pray that *one day God go touch their oppressors*
one day a strange placard appears among a crowd protesting
against all manner of devilish acts emanating from above:
one day the poor will have nothing else to eat but the rich
before you condemn *these hoodlums and hooligans and
miscreants and area boys*
remember the rich
thieves and thugs and their game of greed and graft
the rich as profiteering power-mongers
capitalist exploiters
sellers of people's souls
remember the rich and the rulers destroying the very land
that reared them and expects of them something good in
return.

the rich fathers of the nation resist and reject any change
they desperately hang onto the notion of a nation that is a
big bundle of rumours like a citadel built upon quicksand

and a great entity existing only in the minds of those bandying the lie
the nation has a constitution serving as conduit for corruption
and the very name of the nation was coined by the mistress of the white queen's representative to a land made up of diverse incompatible pieces
yet they have sworn allegiance to the fat lie hoisting them up as heroes in a manner reminding us of the flag of a conqueror over a desert
the rich leaders are courageous only at being cowards
they are patriots only in lining their pockets with loot
they are leaders only at leading the people to ruination
they use forgery and trickery to attain fame
they transform the phenomenon of nation into the pseudomenon of a hell-hole
and change the metamorphosis of nationalities into a powerful singular nation into a pseudomorphosis of village dwellers into a conglomeration of tribes
remember that though tribes and tongues may differ in brotherhood we stand
but remember that tribes exist only in Africa and brotherhood is the call to civil war
the rich and the powerful are souls shackled by psychosis worse than chains confining slaves in the hold of ships heading for civilisation
they will not relent until they drive the people to revolt.

my people, they just don't know
what power they possess
what freedom is and that they must fight for freedom
self-appointed global experts call them the happiest people on earth
they laugh hilariously at everything at nothing for nothing

they easily and willingly adapt to every situation good bad or worse
they complain only to comply and beg and beguile politely and modestly
they turn into dialogue their masters' monologue
by tacit agreement guaranteeing the success of the happy process of dehumanisation
it figures that happy people are hopeless people.

but, yes, my people do know
from revolt will come revolution
revolution has been till date mere rhetoric
it has taken refuge in the cemetery because it is still-born
real revolution, yet unborn, will be a matter of reason and action
a rebirth
a re-invention
a re-invigoration
a return to reality to be transformed into new realisations
our revolution will be televised not in black and white but in living colour
there will be power electrical and socio-political and economic
in the hands of my people
revolution will recognise the enemies inside and outside
who will see themselves in 3-d on their widescreen hi-definition machines
as they and their cronies are being prepared for Armageddon and purgatory on the way to hell
revolution will deal them the blow of you know what
my people will know what it is to suffer and refuse to smile while suffering
they will finally say NO to collaboration with oppressors
NO to despots

NO to hegemonists
NO to killers of my people's dreams
they will know what it is to be free
revolution will nullify all forms of exploitation
particularly their father capitalism
revolution will return power to my people
who are REVOLUTION.

amnesia

we remember the credo:
steal a penny and go to jail
pilfer a pound and get bail
purloin the public funds in billions
and you'll be a hero to millions
yesterday's armed robber may be today's preacher
today's villain may be yesterday's hero
talk of change of fortune
talk of chance
talk of life's inscrutable conditions.

amnesia
is disease doom death denied
corruption clouded by unction
traitors and conspirators eulogised and lionised
as idols and icons
yesterday is dead and long gone
today is a new day
and no matter what people say
the dead can never wake up
nor own up
to their clean or dirty deeds.

amnesia
is to forget to remember
the iniquities of masters of deceit and destruction
the murders and massacres
the manipulations and mismanagement of lives without
hope

Femi Ojo-Ade

the machinations and special arrangements of bodies and minds
the impunity with which dictatorial representatives of the people
changed democracy into deathocracy.

amnesia
is not to forget
but to remember their evil deeds
they think we were are asleep
they think we were are blind
they think we have forgotten will forget
but we will remember
we will remember the injustice of judges
we will remember the incompetence of officers selected or elected by hook or crook
we will remember the indifference of the commander-in-chief to the pain of the people
we will remember
not to ever forget.

poverty

he can't buy food
but he wants to look good
his mind is shallow
his life is hollow.

he can't send his children to school
but he must look cool
he thinks nothing of education
he thinks he can achieve anything by throwing words into
the air.

he blames the leaders for corruption
but he sees nothing wrong in collaboration and collusion
and submission
he says he's oppressed
but his ambition is to become an oppressor
like evil and the devil.

he worships the gods of wealth
in a land of honey turned into a wilderness of misery
where people have become pawns in the desperate gamble
for material
people can't free their mind
people find themselves in a bind
people can't behave like humankind
people are simply unkind.

gods of material
must be put on trial

Femi Ojo-Ade

so that
people can be free
people can see
the dilemma the disease the desolation
of poverty and paucity of body and soul
in a land of plenty turned into a desert of nothingness.

funny
how the constraining constructs of class stand to be
conquered
how conflicts can create space for solidarity
how death can make us cultivate the determination and
desire to defeat
death
even as death hems us in from all sides
steel shattered into dust
metal melted into a mound of rubble and rubbish
men women children
mashed into a metallic mess of flesh and bones
in a union of life and death.

and he still asserts his inability to feed himself
while dreaming big and beaming with an inexplicable pride
not thinking of anything but living the good life
in some paradise here but there and still here
and
at the crossroads of Church and Mosalasi Streets
stands a homeless man
sad but seemingly self-assured
cup in shaking hand
face seared by the heat of the tropical sun
pass some change, ma'am?

beauty

in the beholder's eyes it is
they say
but the beholder may be blind or biased
he may be a fool
he may indeed be a slave to their civilisation
and its universalist standard based upon everything excluding
us.

miss universe
miss world
miss wherever whatever
damsels thin as a pole
devoid of flesh
full of fashion
clad in sheer designer clothes
showing off their endowments
specially ordered from silicone and other valleys of shame and
superficiality
universal standard bought by aspirants to their civilisation.

and the colour comes first and foremost
women with smooth shining skin
in sublime shades of the colour black
black as ebony
black as the colour of Mother Earth
beautiful as legendary queens of our courageous nations
beautiful as new-born babies with soft skin and smiling faces
beautiful as the nature's pristine garden unsullied by
destroyers called developers.

and the colour has changed for the sake of modernity
black has been bastardised
black has been *upgraded* to close to white
black has left the basement for the penthouse
black has shed its low shades to assume the supremacy of white
black women bleach and tone
they bleach and taint
they bleach and tarnish
the colour black.

modern beauty queens
come with bodies toned tanned and tarnished with imported beauty products transforming beauty into a multi-coloured zombie
they must suffer from some brain disease making the veins threaten to burst out of the body and the skin as pale and appalling as the moronic figure of Michael Jackson in his downturn days as the king of pop
their ghostly features would make one vomit
if one were in the habit
of paying attention to such silliness
but one knows that beauty is an international business
and those women must eat.

food by all means necessary
without pride
without self and social awareness
without self-worth
without commitment to culture and country
without shame
food and fashion modern and meaningless
food as source of enslavement of a whole people yet scarred by that unparalleled genocide.

and the search for ugliness continues
on the runways of Europe and Africa
and the world of white wonders
with our women wearing with pride their fanta faces
accompanied by men in masks of mascara like masquerades.

beauty all-inclusive must take care of the crown
the head and hair
symbols of pride and natural quality
and supremacy of the human
black hair soft and kinky
the texture marking and announcing strength and firmness
black hair has been civilised into blonde and many shades but black
it has become long and luscious and sexy and whatever
but black
and black has been caged under a wig when not entwined in human hair
imported from abroad.

and nollywood
is one of the wonders of the world of
beauty.

paradox

(for Ngugi and Njeeri)

yesterday
began the struggle for freedom
as the fathers claimed to have fought and fought and fought
against the missionaries of murder
masked behind the image of their messiah.

yesterday
continued the struggle for freedom
as the fathers of the nation took the baton from the masters
of mayhem
become mentors and still masters of civilisation.

yesterday
transformed the fathers into masters of murder and mayhem
in a land they helped to build and bring down
paradox.

yesterday
became timeless as night and day
coalesce in a conundrum of confusion and
conflict and competition for
things once considered sacred
as commitment to a struggle to save Africa
from marauders from afar and now near
as the inside and outside mesh and merge into
one ball of confusion
paradox.

yesterday
became today as heroes transmuted into villains
still claiming a place in the paradise of their satanism
and capitalism
and bestialism
paradox.

yesterday
saw the exit of sons and daughters concerned with the
unfolding tragedy of independence
and development
and progress
concretised in dependence and defeat and destitution
paradox.

yesterday
saw Ngugi wa Thi'ongo and Micere Mugo blaze the trail of
exile
to escape death
to energise the heart and soul of commitment and protest
to live with the masters
to collaborate
to copy
to lean on or learn from them?
masters
enemy
missionaries of murder and mayhem?
paradox.

yesterday
became today
years after yesterday
mother of today
exile and its sorrow

Femi Ojo-Ade

exile and its sadness
exile and its paradox
exile and its perplexity
exile as exit from hell into heaven
exile as combination of good and ill health
exile as heaven and hell
exile and its mental travails and material triumphs
paradox.

yesterday and today and tomorrow
Africa's dilemma of doom
you left to return home some day as today
escape from yesterday's hell
into today's heaven as murderous as yesterday's hell
paradox.

yesterday's exit
today's entry
yesterday's departure
today's return
yesterday's hopelessness
today's hope riddled with hammer blows to both heart and
soul
reminder that past and present represent the same reality
of rape and repression and oppression
paradox.

today
one came back home with his dear wife
to savour the love of the land
to reconnect with his roots
to be and live again Africa
but he forgot that Africans are now modern and mean and
murderous and

ever ready to eliminate anyone at any time
for a pittance or a pile of filthy material
the uninvited welcome party came to the five-star hotel with weapons
to pump bullets into the dumbfounded couple.

and today
there are
the people
the people as pawn in the political game of powerful gangsters
the powerful as mentors of the oppressed
the people as handmaids of the powerful
the people as collaborators of criminals
Africa's destiny
paradox.

obamaphobia

run, Obama run, run, run!
and he ran through minefields
set by monstrous minnows
run, Obama, run, run, run!
and he ran and ran and ran
making hope become change
to the dismay of those forever saying nay
they tried to run him to the ground
still he ran and ran and ran
until he forced open the locked gate of their white house
not as cook or butler or servant
but as
president of these United States of America!

Obama
as symbol of success elixir panacea for all woes and sorrows
as passport to paradise on earth
as harbinger of hope and happiness
as symbol of post-racial America
really?

hawkers of hate shouted themselves hoarse:
not in these united states!
ghosts of past madness rose from the grave
birthers and teapartiers come baiting and bullying
spitting spite embedded in a complex of superiority
they unfurl the star-spangled banner tainted and tattered
with branding and lynching as their covert goals
are hidden behind images of patriotism and nationalism

and love for an America etched in their memories of days of control
of oppression and repression of their slaves
some even display the flag of confederacy flush with black blood
spilled on the battlefields of unity tainted with the selfish pursuits
of plantation masters
love of America, no!
love of liberty, no!
love of people, no!
love of power, oh, yes!

modern madness it is
civilised craziness it is
it is built upon hypocrisy and arrant hatred
it is the politics of power
obamaphobia is the latest americophilia
of stark racism bracketed with traditional supremacism
it is in full flight with afropessimism
expressive of racism creator and cultivator of slavery and colonialism
with Africa as victim of the genocide and the barbarity misconstrued as
civilisation
obama osama whatever his name is
obasama haughty and naughty
shucking and jiving and shuffling and jive-tuckeying nigger!
obama the retard
the drone driver destroying humanity
the kenyan terrorist
the Oluwole Street birth certificate and passport forger
osama's illegitimate brother and al-qaeda collaborator

the jihadist joker selling off America's civilised soul
to muslim fundamentalists
the embodiment of all things un-American.

and the racist rage and disrespect continue:
sit down and shut up, liar!
commands a filthy-mouthed loose canon
to the commander-in-chief in full public glare
*to place a white republican in the white house
is not to be racist but to be a true American!
we are ruled by a communist who bows down to allah
obama is a dunce, absolutely!
he's a food-stamp president
he hates america
america the beautiful america the bountiful*

*why does obama hate america?
the alien the terrorist the socialist
the communist the un-american
the african
we must ship him back to the jungle in kenya!*

the dog has moved from being underdog to top dog
says one goon trying to be funny
dog as hunting in the jungle
underdog as in slaves on the plantation
top dog as in their capital and their white house
that's why he has to follow his master's orders
like being a good nigger
like being a smiling savage
like being a big black baby bending politely
and whispering yessuh massa with his eyes flush with
fear.

thus unfolds the unabated sing-song of americanism by
intellectual paperweights pretending to be intelligent heavy-
hitters
callous cynics accusing a patriot of patricide
genocidists and nihilists yelling murder against a humanist
lynch mobs hunting down character and colour black
deaf as they are to reason and incapable of distinguishing
right from wrong
sad imitation of people protesting against forces of
occupation and oppression
modern defenders of deception adept at the trickery of
images of phantom reality.

yet Obama stands strong
the gait of the God-sent
the conduct of the committed
the mastery of mass movement
the love of America
the conviction of communal cooperation
the dignity the daring the decisiveness
the hope beyond the wildest dreams of hawkers of hate
the belief that America will outlive the suffocating scenario
of destruction and descent to the hell that will engulf the
purveyors of doom
that is the supremacy of the man in America's white house
the house constructed by slaves and their children.

Femi Ojo-Ade

a fall from grace

from prince to pimp to prostitute
it is but a short simple step
from president to pirate
from patriot to pariah
it is but a matter of minutes
such is Africa's experience with
ruthless rulers and
dastardly dictators
determined to perpetuate themselves in power
as if they can kill death
as they murder the mass of their people.

their faces tell the tale of tragedy
as they mutate slowly but surely
from the beautiful to the beastly
from force to fear
from pride and pomposity to the sick and the sunken
the lion feared for its ferocity
transmutes into a lame duck ducking and dodging
bullets and bazookas
a deflated bird caught in a cage facing imminent death
blinking and bowing before those that dared
not look him in the eye only days before
dazed like a prisoner dragged from the dark dungeon into
the blinding light
don't kill me, please!
the first and only words of a shameless criminal.

the dividends of democracy
crafted by the con artist crossover from the halls of academe:
men sprayed with petrol burnt and beaten to death
bodies disintegrating under the excited gaze of a crowd in ecstasy
people scampering off with arms raised as sign of peace and solidarity
or simple submission before death?

the prince become pauper of power
sits with his spouse and crime partner
gazing at nothing
still trying to look powerful
even though his posture is exposed
like the backside of a king stripped naked in the market place.

suddenly appeared a man from
nowhere
to deliver a dirty double slap to the face of
the prince.
silence.

religion

pompous priests
prurient pastors
prayerful preachers
prey upon their guilty and gullible congregation
in the name of
Money and Material
and
Power and Prosperity.

his holiness ditched his bicycle his volkswagen his mercedes
for
a jet
purchased with tithes paid by his poverty-riddled
congregation and
various visitors from high on the national rock of robbers
because the pastor's movement must be fast and furious
against
the devil
and all those wreaking havoc on the hopes of redemption of
God's innocent children
because the priest cannot afford to be poor
when the Almighty has decreed riches for the righteous
because the leader must lead by example.

the preacher hides behind the veil of valour
he sermonises against sin and sophistry and
decadence and desecration of the holy and
defamation of the virtuous representations of God's religion
yet

away from the pulpit and the probing eyes of the public
the man of God
sins and steals and
fornicates and deals in myriad filthy fiendish acts
in the company of his friends up on the rock of robbers.

for pastor priest preacher
religion is the road to riches
means of making good money
source of strength to control and kill popular conscience
passport to the paradise living grandly in their pockets.

for the poor and powerless
religion is succour from suffering
means of escaping misery
spiritual security
reason to avoid responsibility and
to ask the Almighty to take charge
of lost lives and forsaken fate and hopeless hope.

so pastor priest preacher
pounces on the made to order prey
without a sense of shame
without thinking of God
without thinking
as the jet soars towards the skies
and suddenly dives towards the unforgiving earth.

north and south

the north points upwards
far far away above the earth
the south points downwards
deep deep down into the earth.

the north is home to Europeans
and others
the south is home to Africans
and others
the colonisers from up there
and
their colonised down here
came together in a conflict of cultures
with vultures capturing treasures
and
their victims living according to their whims.

then came independence and its dependence
the north transmuted from masters to mentors
the south changed from colonised to
colluders and collaborators and collaterals
and
both became allies in the global village
and
the north keeps soaring towards the skies
and
the south keeps struggling to survive
in a game of unequals with unequal opportunities.

paradise points upwards
hell downwards
north remains above
south below
both separated by the space
between life and death
so says the cynical mad man
who fled the mental institution and
declared that the president of his nation
should be the first inmate.

bolt

(for Usain Bolt)

he is a gangly giant with the gait of a gazelle
he dominates the field with speed and grace
he is the bolting bolt
lightning bolt
easing slowly out of the blocks
but surely catching the fast starters
with the sudden speed of a freight train
with the unleashed fury of a rocket targeted at evil
in a sport once symbolic of sheer talent grace and integrity
now being smeared by the antics of sophisticated cheats
bent upon being the best by all means necessary.

from adolescent to adult
bolt has traced the trajectory of excellence
manifested
cultivated
controlled
to the point of supremacy
at eighty meters of the sprint
he is abreast of the now plodding pacesetters aspiring to be
bolt beaters
suddenly forced to freeze in full flight
like robots customised by computer gurus
to whet human hopes to control machines
representing, always to our ignorance, our worst nightmares.

so here comes bolt fast as a supersonic
pushing aside the pretenders to a throne made for the one
candidate with all the necessary attributes of

skill
speed
charismatic force
controlled fury
disarming confidence
earthy demeanour
the grace of those gliding strides
the beguiling grin in those darting eyes
the subtle sign of affirmed superiority
as the giant blows past his opposition
the separation strikes like lightning
on the tracks of our times.

tell me about Jesse Owens and that speed
and the fortitude to conquer the force of nazism
tell me about Carlos and Smith standing up for Black against racism
tell me about others fighting for freedom
but, please, tell me also about
Bolt
and the hope of times out of darkness into
the light of a new day
tell me again about that
spectacular speed
to run away from modern prisons and plantations
to run through mighty barriers and barricades and biases
to run to true freedom.

one day in America

the sun was shining bright and beautiful
the weather was warm and wonderful
the skies were smiling with joy and
the people were all awash with happiness and harmony
on a day unique in its political correctness.

I saw princes and paupers bunched together in the warmth
of a weird winter
waiting to hail their black president
I saw love fulfilled in eyes filled with tears
I saw men and women and young and old clinging together
and looking in one direction
I saw humans hugging one another congratulating one
another with the innocence of new birth.

and one day in Africa?
the sun shines brighter than in America
but the glow stops at skin level
Nigeria with graft and greed stomping upon the people's soul
Kenya with neocolonial antagonism enmeshed in power
hunger and cultural conundrum
Mali and Central Africa with their miasma of religious
fundamentalism and national alienation
South Africa with the stifling shadow of apartheid clogging
the spirit of the confused nationalists
Zimbabwe with heroic guerilla hoarding power for a gang of
gerontocratic goons.

and some day in Africa?
maybe Nigeria would finally transmute into a nation
maybe Kenya would find its mettle again as the refined centre of Africa's forward movement
maybe Mali and Central Africa would rise again to the age-old heights of cultural excellence
maybe South Africa would fulfill Mandela's promise of freedom and progress for the people
maybe Zimbabwe would re-affirm the quality of commitment and the true definition of heroism.

one day in America
they eschewed enmity
they exorcised the demon of democratic recklessness fixated upon
rights
the right to hate
the right to hound
the right to haunt
their perceived enemy and alien
being black.

one day in America
they all showed love for
Obama!

Africa, my Africa

You are the mother of the world
The cradle of culture and civilisation
You're not homeland but home
To innumerable children whose past and present and future
remain forever attached to your soul
You symbolise impeccable beauty of heart and soul
Unmatchable are your humility and generosity
Qualities that have been rather problematic
In a world mired in selfishness and spite for
You and your offspring
In a world where your colour and culture are vilified without
respite.

Detractors call you abominable names
Stereotypy is an excellent ideology, and act of genius.
Ape-Baboon-Monkey-Gorilla
God's chosen arbiters of human fate and behaviour cannot be queried or quarried.
Savage-Beast-Cannibal
You're roundly guilty until proven innocent.
Heathen-Pagan-Atheist
It's the magnanimous mission of the civilised to snatch the savages from the jaws of their living hell and uplift them toward Civilisation and our heaven on earth.
Ignorant-Infidel-Irresponsible
We know them, they are born and bred like that; they can never, will never, change.
Criminal-Cretin-Rapist

The perceived *sins of the parents shall be visited upon the children.*
Darkness-Doom-Death
To be civilised means to be hypocritical, better, to be hateful, best, to be hell-bent on harming, hounding the Other to death, to annul his existence, to reduce him to the level of the beast, to eject him from the human race.
Dark Continent
To place premium on White, to consider White superior, supreme, is not to be racist but realistic, absolutely.
Raw Power-Instinct
All brawn, no brain; all ignorance, no intelligence, like animals.
The odour of the jungle, nauseating, foul, numbing
I can smell them from a distance. That odour cannot be conquered by any perfume or deodorant. No wonder they sleep in the shower, or the wisest of them don't bother to take a shower.
Big Babies-Barbaric-Backward
They act like innocent and naïve children in need of direction and education; they keep smiling and laughing like fools, simpletons that they are.

Big babies, really?
Backward and barbaric, really?
Yet we know your history and heritage
You gave the world a civilisation stolen by others without acknowledgement
You welcomed in good faith visitors from afar that turned out to be enemies
Marauding murderers and genocidal goons
Imperialistic exploiters and irreducible exterminators
Savages hiding under the guise of civilisers.

Your children fell victim to the machinations of the masters of death
From slavery to colonialism
From independence to neocolonialism
From then until now
The same story of your demise and humiliation through your children
Those whose ancestors were uprooted and transplanted into the new world of enslavement
Now praise the Lord and the overlords of the modern plantation for salvation from savagery
They now claim to be scions of the best and brightest extracted from the jungle of jackasses
They are Americans as in masters of the universe
As in the greatest nation on God's earth
As in the police of the world
They forget you, Africa
Their roots, their beginning and their end, their source of strength, their inalterable identity
Particularly in their society still rooted in blatant racism against you and your children.

Your children at home
Are they any better?
The bitter truth tells a story of shame
As millions are caught in a continuously twisted web of oppression and repression
In the hands of pranksters claiming to be patriots
Criminals clad in national colours of theoretical hope and development
Stealing while luring the people to sleep
Leading them to the precipice that they call paradise
Working hand in glove with former masters become mentors.

Your children at home
Are so dejected
So debilitated
So desiccated
That they see their only hope for survival away from home
Thus the new millennium is witnessing a second wave of potential slaves
Then unwilling, now willing and able,
Then traumatised by the experience, now elated to be
on boat or balloon to the security and safety of the Euro-American haven
Then nostalgic for you, Africa, now numb or negative toward any thought of
You, Africa,
Mother tainted with shame by the behaviour of her shameless children
Mother taken aback by the impunity of rulers of the world engaged in a programme of incessant degradation and disgrace of a civilisation toward which they should show gratitude.

Africa,
My Africa,
Notwithstanding today's conundrum following yesterday's conquest
Notwithstanding the foreigners' mass murders physical and psychological
Notwithstanding incessant racist bashing and concerted efforts at balkanisation
Notwithstanding the travesty and temerity of carpetbaggers tracing the pinnacle of the universe to the portals of Buckingham Palace and the White House
Notwithstanding your frontline children's criminality and collaboration with killers of our dreams

Notwithstanding the hordes of refugees penned in camps worse than garbage dumps and pig-sties
Notwithstanding the tragedy of these homeless-helpless-harmless desperately hugging their skeletons of children as they flee the angry fire of guns toted by spaced-out monsters obsessed with power and wealth
Notwithstanding the cloud of death hanging over our tropical skies
We love you
We honour you
We will forever be your loving children
Because we are not bastards denying their home and seeking refuge like homeless hobos
Because we are proud of our identity and heritage
Because without you we are nothing and
Because we insist upon our humanity beginning with the fact of our
Africanity.

civilisation

I cannot play the piano
I cannot stand classical music
I cannot dance ballet
I cannot play golf
I cannot swim.

I no know i-pad or i-pod or i-phone or i-whatever
I just know that I must be one with my people
I am me and my people are me, too
because without others one is nothing.

You say I'm inferior to you
I say I'm equal to you
You say you're superior to me
I say you're inferior to me.

I say I'm superior to you
because I am far greater than
one
and I belong to Africa
Mother and father of all civilisations.

thanksgiving

a time it is should be
to be thankful for all we've got
been given
so we give and receive
material and money
exchange is no robbery
it is human to give and take.

yet we pay too much attention to giving and taking
which could be robbery or worse
when it's a question of having or not
in a context close to and for the soul
bordering on the moral and immoral.

it's thanksgiving
so we give thanks
we gather together in rare family reunion
we devour turkey and other delicious offerings
we shop until shops shut down for lack of merchandise
we shop until we risk dropping dead
we pay no mind to history.

history is hated by hypocrites
hiding their dark secrets with outrageously fantastic fallacies
built upon outlandish fancies
turning truth on its head
designing another story
crafted into pseudo-tales of heroism and magnanimity
in a setting where the least concern is human dignity.

the history of thanksgiving is a tragic tale
unknown to the teeming descendants of the first
transgressors of the vaunted
new world
the tale told or unheeded underscores the evolution of
America into a state
built upon the subjection and submission of every and any
person non-white
the First Americans —they called them red — were picture-
perfect hosts to the colonists
lost during their mission of conquest camouflaged as
civilisation
red helped white
red led white
red saved white
red and white were partners in the progressive pact of
pacification of the wild land
white suddenly turned red into savage to be pacified by
weapons of mass destruction
in the unilaterally established hierarchy of supremacism
white supreme master of the universe
white superior to red
white superior to all others
black was lucky to live long
because he was essential commodity for constructing the
new white citadel
red was destined to disappear
in the programme of insult and assault unconsciously aided
and abetted by black
red survivors were relegated to reservations
while black slaves were penned in plantations.

history never lies
even if it is often used to tell lies
as thanksgiving tells the new history of the master's
hardiness and heroism
transforming First American simple but soulful meal of
gratitude
into a sumptuous feast of excessive magnitude
replacing familiar figures of family and community
with images of bacchanal and epicurean magnanimity
modest meals and humble minds
are replaced by material and money
the power of plenty
supplants the humility of the heart
thanksgivers flaunt the filth of abundance
in the face of poverty and homelessness
they eat and eat and eat
they throw out the left-over for horses and in the garbage
while freezing millions are starving and seeking a meal in
shelters.

thanksgiving is a day of joy
but the First Americans know the ploy
as they remember how their heritage day
now named Black Friday
tells another tale of their tragedy
Friday is black
 because the colour contrasts with red
black connoting success
red signifying failure
black showing that you're in financial heaven on earth
red implying condemnation to material mess
Friday is the day after thanksgiving
when you shop until you drop
when you pay homage to the gods of capitalism

when you show your appreciation of materialism
when you prove your allegiance to Americanism
when you revel in the new life on Wall Street
out of the ghetto
out of the slums
out of the cold
out of the bottom of the ladder.

Friday may also be black
because the model shopper is supposedly black
addicted to designer articles
connoisseur of classy clothes
yet victim of shopping while black
thus reminding him of his place in the paradise on Main Street
yet he savours the one day when black can escape bigotry
biological bias and social stigmatisation
negative notions and stereotyping.

and the First Americans are cooling their heels at the corner of side streets
and they are mumbling something strange under their breath
as merry-makers filled with the mirth of thanksgiving are telling them to chill and join the parade.

from across the ocean come calls of congratulations
happy thanksgiving, everyone!
from many African countries that many residents of America call home
calls always come on thanksgiving
on labour day
on mother's day
on father's day

on president's day
on every special day
as if America's day is Africa's designated day
like counterfeit imitating the real deal
like servant aping master
images of past and present
when civilisers past and present
carry out their mission of manipulation and imposition
as they educate us to appreciate the good things of life
outside Africa
as decreed from above in America.

we celebrate thanksgiving
even if we do not know its history
after all we are dismissive of our history
best left to corrode
not to explode
because we must exude the joy of living
even if it's all about living a lie.

thanksgiving is turkey day
the bigger the bird the better the delicacy
turkey in Africa is an expensive commodity
you pay for a skinny bird with an arm and a leg
no wonder one woman travelling home from America
had the wonderful idea of exporting turkey home:
she packed a box full of birds
she was looking forward to a season of joy with thanksgiving
stretching to Christmas
then she collapsed just as the plane began its final descent to
land at home.

rather than playing turkey
let us find common ground with America's founding fathers

whose desires
echo the age-old dictates of our ancestors and elders
we must show gratitude
for being alive with humility and no attitude
we must be thankful for survival
we must aspire toward revival
of our sorry society in need of a communion
we must operate from the basis of a genuine union
for the benefit of our people
happy thanksgiving, y'all!

Haiti

a woman — ebony black oozing the beauty of Africa's soul —
stands teary-eyed amidst a muddy mess of dilapidation
a child — stark naked, innocent-looking with teeth glowing
like the sun- sits among the jumbled rubble, clutching a
wingless toy plane and crying shrilly for his absent parents
crowds of people — visibly all shades of dark- are coming
and going nowhere in the thick smoke of still burning
remains of rickety buildings consumed by hurricane
Freedom in conjunction with fires of mysterious sources.

Haiti is a country irretrievably riven and driven toward
destruction by human callousness
keep the poor on a diet of disease
but keep them from dying if you can
keep them in their temporary yet timeless shacks with no
running water no electricity in a marshland of mud and
flood.

Haiti is under the murderous grip of a second natural
disaster in as many years
it's a disaster inevitable but at once baffling in its seriousness
and sequence
in a small island whose physical perfection and political
programme and aspiration were truncated by the invasion
and occupation by Spain aided by local racist hegemonists.

Haiti has lost is losing millions of innocent victims
its land is being transformed into a wilderness of devastation
and a den of disease

Femi Ojo-Ade

by the combined action of nature and man
while the sea vents its anger on the land
while structures collapse like afflicted weaklings and falling mosquitoes trapped by insecticides
while villages are deserted by perplexed humans running helter-skelter and finding solace in shelters becoming deadly cages before their very eyes.

Haiti is a victim not only of hurricane Freedom and earthquake Fiefdom
but also of human hurricanes and typhoon-like tycoons and monstrosities in the aftermath
all adducible to the almighty international community represented by the United Nations and non-governmental organisations and various nations and individual sympathisers
each functioning like the legendary tortoise witty and tardy in their involvement
they act as if Haiti were a laboratory experiment with ample time for the researchers' reflection
they act as if misery and disease are waiting to be eradicated over a lifetime
with no immediacy no urgency no pressure.
individuals including exiled Haitians that have set up shop to collect and use cash for a rescue mission are reputedly doing more for their pockets than the people.

we cannot over-emphasise the deadly events
even if we were to retell the tale a million times over
human propensity to self-destruct is matched, nay, overmatched by nature's one-stroke demolition
not once but twice
suddenly the earth begins to shake — human made by greedy oil companies, assert some accusatory voices —

then turns everyone and everything upside down
and sinks one and all in a hell-hole of rubble and rubbish
then, only months later, before the dust has settled on the
pulverised and perished humans and earth
there comes another deadly hit by nature
from angered waters hell-bent on reclaiming the land being
wasted and wantonly abused by shallow-minded humans
the hurricane lands out of season
it sweeps every fragile being and object in its path
and Haiti once again becomes mourning and mourned
widower widow orphan.

outrageous criticism and condemnation reign supreme
according to the rules of the global capitalist game of
grandstanding and gullibility
most striking and strident is the voice of the self-anointed
fathers of christian decadence averring that the natural
disasters are deserved retribution and restitution for Haiti's
past abomination of voodoo
that Haitians are now paying the price for their temerity in
dining with the devil and for myriad sins against God
that God has chosen His time to concretise His curse upon
the inveterate sinners and sons and daughters of satan.

only the foolish congregation of those hypocritical cohort
would believe that lie by
those that keep the Bible closed and use it as mask for their
life of iniquities or read it upside down
those that quote the good book out of context
those that work for the devil in the name of God
those that use it to conquer souls into slavery and to colonise
in the name of civilisation.

Haiti herself must share in the blame of human criminality
even though the masters of the world are, as usual, the main perpetrators
Haiti, once the power in control of the whole island of Hispaniola,
is now subordinate and subservient to the Dominican Republic founded upon the principle of white and mulatto supremacism
Haitians willingly provided the workforce that built the Dominican nation
that now declares illegal and illegitimate not only those deserving of national honours
but their descendants born and bred on the modern slave plantation.
Dominica has benefited from the racist act of a concert of colonisers:
Spain, France and the United States have succeeded in bouncing Haiti back to its place as pariah and pauper
further punishment it is for her impunity in winning the war against her oppressor France in addition to the millions of dollars levied against her
Haiti took a whole century to buy an underhanded victory
till today deemed a loss undeserving of any respect by the *civilised* world
Haiti plummeted like a free-falling craft in distress crashing to the bottom of the sea of slavery
and she has since not stopped suffering from typhoon Tyranny and earthquake Corruption.

today's tragedy makes many forget the past triumph of the Revolution
arguably one of the world's greatest anti-colonial victories
when puny minnow Haiti snatched her freedom from the jaws of powerful mighty France

voodoo was the anchor of the revolutionary movement
stoked by the faith and fire of such heroic houngans as
Makandal and Boukman
voodoo was the vital component at the core of commitment
based upon integrity of community
voodoo revived the contents of culture
voodoo revitalised faith in the Supreme Being as source of
strength to struggle for freedom
voodoo demanded and obtained confidentiality of action
voodoo was sacred and sublime and hard-core, conscious
and conscientious, focused upon liberation as an inevitable
goal not by happenstance under any circumstance but by
unshakable resolve
without voodoo the Revolution would have failed.

pivotal it was that Toussaint Louverture revered father of the
nation proved his superiority
pivotal too that his successor Dessalines maintained his
integrity
no less pivotal was Christophe's insistence on his Africanity
yet
the three fathers of the nation exemplify the tragedy of the
Revolution:
they compromised their culture by a cop-out to the
christianising mission of the masters
they vilified voodoo
they desecrated the shrines of our deities
they accepted western savagery under the cloak of
civilisation
no wonder Toussaint was betrayed and bundled into the
hold of a ship bound for his mountain prison in France
no wonder Dessalines was assassinated by the collusion of
his own black followers and the mulattoes

no wonder the abandoned Christophe took the shameful option of suicide.

in essence, the Revolution fizzled out under the onslaught of chaos and collaboration of criminals
not to forget the coercion choreographed by the almighty west
the post-Revolution saw Haiti back in the throes of sectarianism and racial divide
Black stood against Mulatto
and they both forgot the patriotic energy that drove the Revolution to victory
when, later, they again listened to the voice of Haiti calling them to order
it was too late to obliterate the vestiges of ego-tripping and racial hegemony.

post-Christophe Haiti became a banana republic of overnight rulers
reminiscent of one-night standers in rundown hotel rooms
too much bombastic blabber by puny politicians fresh out of military uniform
too many gun-toting goons among the mass of meek a-political citizens
too much autocracy in a country built upon the strength of communal consensus
too little commitment in a society where conscience and consciousness were at the core of the hard-won freedom from bondage.

Haiti has had almost fifty heads of state since the Revolution
many have been turn-coat military masters with no notion of nation
some have benefited from nepotism

others have been privileged by racism
all have failed to achieve the greatness once attained by Haiti
now as far away as heaven from hell.

Haiti has also suffered from the confusion of racial identity and definition
with the clearer designations of black and mulatto being replaced by the more confusing constructs of
black-dark-light
whereby there is room for argument and disagreement
and opposition and failure to progress
in a land where black remains at the bottom of the ladder
notwithstanding the number of designations
notwithstanding the desire to fool and be fooled
notwithstanding the many attempts to hide the racial cankerworm.

prominent among modern Haiti's presidents are the Duvaliers
papa doc and baby doc epitomise sick misrulers raising the banner of bastardy to high heavens
they used religion to regale themselves and relegate the mass to the level of the rubble consequential to the earthquake devastating all in sight
papa died and then his disgraced tyrant-traitor-tycoon son flew away to the comfortable confines of his French Riviera castle
in the exclusive enclave of dictators and despots
democratically supported by France.

prominent, too, is Aristide
for being a commie
a word defined in the west's lexicon as a true leader
committed to his people's cause

a leader daring to stand up against the almighty imperialists
a leader refusing to dance in the arena of modern plantocracy
a leader focused on his people's freedom and his country's development
Aristide was sent packing into exile in South Africa
While Haiti was handed over to pimping presidents of colours of the rainbow
including the current musician Sweet Micky famous for censoring anti-government bands from the annual carnival
as if — so say civilised observers- all that matters to the people is song and dance in celebration of their misery.

noteworthy it is that the face and voice of Haiti's leader are unseen unheard
amidst the rubble and rumblings of earthquake and hurricane
the status quo has been restored
peace on earth and poverty in Haiti
scenes of sorrow and suffering in places pulverised by agents of death
Belair, with its poisoned air belying the beauty bestowed upon the land by nature suddenly outraged by humans' heinous crimes
Cité-Soleil, and the sham sun of shame, where the sun once radiant and shining its exquisite light upon a people poor yet proud and rich in their dignity and integrity, has been subdued by forces of darkness transforming happiness into helplessness
Jacmel, where the crush of crowds once made one's heart sing with joy, appears to be a space occupied by ghosts, where honey tastes like poison and love bears affinity to hate, and
Port-au-Prince, symbolic entrance to a land fit for royalty

and the splendour of a paradise now fallen into disgrace and
wrapped in squalour best suited for hell.

Haitians are seeking refuge and solace in others' homes
they are wanderers of the world
nomads of the south heading north
working so that the north's machine of domination may
function in perfection
they stand toiling endlessly so that others may sit in comfort
they sit on cue so that others may stomp upon their supine
bodies
they are their niggers, so think the masters.

Haitians are our brothers in bondage and our sisters in a
struggle
compromised by circumstances seemingly beyond our
control
we are migrants desperate to die on the Mediterranean
we are destitute travellers in the Sahara serving as our
sprawling cemetery
we are willing slaves overloading ship-holds and the bellies
of various beasts of the skies
just to kiss the hallowed soil of almighty Euro-America
yet our dreams are too often left to rot and flounder in the
tumultuous tides of hurricanes and typhoons
in a scenario where reactionary Cubans fleeing their nation
are given a red-carpet welcome
Haitians are hounded and forced to head back home to
misery
and one has memories of the past feeding the present
with Black pinned down under the master's boots
strung up on a tree
toiling away in the plantation
serving as the Other's carpet or stepping stone.

Haiti — they call it the poorest nation in the western hemisphere- is eking out a living
bare-boned back-breaking bleak, fretting from the dark still clouds enveloping the atmosphere just before the seismic shock shattering the tranquility of a place once as beautiful as pristine Africa
Haiti's reeling from the bazooka blows of hurricane Fiefdom and earthquake Corruption
the philanthropists are in retreat because other victims need aid
meanwhile we remember that the great organ of united universal commitment and concern
inadvertently contaminated Haiti with a devastating cholera epidemic
without acknowledgement
without accepting responsibility
without a sense of urgency to save dying children and adults.

Haiti must be grateful that anybody cares
Haiti must be thankful that the mighty and powerful have paid attention
Haiti must blame none other than herself for her misfortune
Haiti and her people
no streets are named after them
no monuments are erected in their memory
no chapter in history books is devoted to their heroism
they cannot even read
if and when they can read
there are no books to read.

at a McDonald's in the American capital
sits a blonde blue-eyed buxom bombshell
sipping coke with a double-whopper burger waiting to be coaxed into submission

she exudes compassion as the television runs a show on the plight of Haiti
hardly opening her mouth plastered with flaming red lipstick, she whispers:
I just love Haiti!

all about us and them

contrast of colours
white skin white masks
black skin white masks
black is an absence
white is a presence
on the world's power scheme
globalisation and its first-worldism
neocolonialism and its third-worldism.

memories of worldism past developing into
the present of black woes and
white wonders
from pre-colonial to post-colonial Africa
independence became perpetual dependence
aptly named partnerships in progress
whereby we regress
as they progress
and trample upon our soil and soul.

they eradicated our freedom
and established a new serfdom
reminiscent of slavery
partnerships in progress
aid to the developing underdeveloped
civilisation for the uncivilised
delivery of democracy to the undemocratised
such is the master's sermon on the mountain of modernity
shared with Africa's leaders as chosen by the almighty
through the masters
working for themselves their acolytes in collusion against us
the people.

a national incident
(for victims of bomb attack)

we were given ample warning to worry
but not to worry
by authorities never in control of
a land they claim to lead and to love.

the good people of the place they call bountiful and beautiful
and peaceful
and born to be among the best ever constructed by God's
chosen civilisers
the good people should pay no mind to cynical criminals and
devilish dream-killers
even if they see neither proof of progress rather a progressive
record of retrogression
even when the leaders are liars and lynching leeches
even if the commonly recognised illogic is posited in our
paradise as logic
even when the stinking air is suffused with the odour of
death.

the day of reckoning came and went
the moment of expectation arrived and waned
the clock of death ticked and tocked
and wound down beyond the feared hour of national horror.

the good people with the good government
jumped for joy
danced and drank
with bulging backsides shaking to the afrobeat offered by
bad imitators of the original sound

with teeth shining white like the snow civilising our enslaved ancestors' confused souls
just like the day of independence ushering the dawn of new dependence.

then, suddenly came the surreal second
bang bang bang in succession
right there at Independence Square
only seconds after mr. father of the nation had departed the scene of celebration
bodies piled upon bodies
like slaves stacked in the hold waiting to ship out to
the eternal glory of the new world civilisation.

bodies breathless
bodies lifeless
bodies once beautiful
bodies once hopeful
even in their hopelessness
bodies uncountable
bodies providing good reason for another official lie
the all-knowing authorities announced the number
twenty
yet a blind man could confirm that it was in several multiples of
twenty.

we don't need to worry about numbers
they lie all the time
they the critics the nihilists the prophets of doom
they cannot fathom the patriotic passion of our devoted leaders
God's chosen shepherds
leading us to the promised land of

Independence Square
where our destiny is a done deal
of death
death in this vale of sorrow and sacrifice
necessary prelude to life everlasting in
paradise
the illogic for hell.

living while black

looking while black
walking while black
talking while black
shopping while black
driving while black
fighting while black
that's how their jaundiced eyes see us
because we're the visible and vulnerable other
on the street on the subway
at the airport at the train station
everywhere
Black is a stain on the human landscape
where dogs are deemed and treated better than Black.

Amadou Diallo was opening his apartment's door
for which four officers of the law pumped over forty bullets
into
his black body backing the street
the officers were committed to public safety
they thought the boy had a gun endangering their innocent
lives and
the wise judge acquitted them.

Renisha McBride went to a nearby house in search of
assistance after
a car accident that spared her life
her reward was a bullet to the face by the home owner
explaining his act as
accidental discharge of a gun that he shot point blank

straight at the target
black being to his mind an unwanted accident on the face of the earth.

James Byrd was picked up by three morons white as snow on the outside but dark as death
on the inside
and they tied him to the rear of their terror truck and dragged him down the dirt road
that shredded his body like a blender or a machine reducing solid mass to a meaningless mess
the drunken trio went to a bar to booze away their bold-faced elimination of
a black man deemed unfit to exist in a world that must belong solely to them.

Trayvon Martin was sighted armed with a hoodie and trailed by a self-appointed vigilante chief
because he was guilty of being black and therefore a criminal to be erased from
the civilised neighbourhood reserved for white and wannabes
the vigilante disregarded the police order not to follow the innocent young man
who must have wondered why the chase and why the attack
that left him dead of a bullet shot in self-defense by the only armed man
in the struggle that led to acquittal of the guilty vigilante congratulated for ridding the streets of civilisation of another
Black.

Emmett Till young and innocent accused of whistling at a white woman

was caught tortured lynched and drowned in the murky waters of Mississippi
by a mob of white masters of murder and madness
in a state known for its racism and retrogression
no wonder it took years to mete justice to the victim's family and punish the mob
because poor Emmett and his people are considered a black blight on the pale face of almighty America.

Trayon Christian saved his paltry dollars and cents to purchase a prized designer belt
Kayla Phillips did the same to purchase an expensive purse
only to be stopped and searched and hounded and humiliated by
staff and security of a departmental store reputed for treating humans with dignity
while Black is considered hardly human and at best on the outskirts of the lily-white community
Black cannot afford high quality stuff because we are born poor and penniless!
Black must have stolen that belt and that purse because we are born pick-pockets!!
because we are slaves to material and servants to the masters that we imitate as they initiate
us into the wonderful world of riches and treasures that we cannot acquire except by
stealing!!!

we talk black they say
because we are born illiterate and
our umbilical cord remains chained to our ancestors from the jungle
where language remains a dialect of the backward cousins of the simian species

from the dark continent to the white new world came the
best and brightest
who still could not climb the ladder to the top
because of their barbaric antecedents that prevented them
from learning to speak proper English
their Ebonics is nothing but garbled speech patterns
underscoring the basic confusion
of a people incapable of clarity and dignity and
responsibility.

we fight while black
as a community committed to contributing to the
construction of a nation
as a people immersed in patriotism and in the struggle for
justice and peace
in a world troubled by terrorism and victim of vicious crimes
against humanity
yet the self-appointed masters of the universe never let us
forget that
black is a stigma for second-class citizenship and colour of
the lowest on the ladder
segregated units and battalions commanded by petty white
officers
achieved extraordinary exploits on the battlefield only to be
treated later with opprobrium
their virtue was dumped in the mud by racist vitriol and
viciousness
their accomplishments were debunked by overbearing cant
and contempt
as it was in the past so it is in the present
Black remains an outsider in a society built by his blood and
sweat
and war for him is a constant synonym for peace
as both signify struggle for survival on the verge

where reality is the absence of existential essentials
where being black is a bane
even when the myth of liberty and equality and justice rings
out from the top of the mountain.

fame would be a means of dodging the dilemma of profiling
small or big-screen superstars and box-office busters would
be the exception to
living while black
they'd be honorary whites just living their sweet lives in
peace
alas, reality debunks such alluring naiveté and hollow hope.

ask the oscar-winning Forest Whitaker frisked in a deli for
being
black
ask the billionaire Oprah Winfrey denied the right to see a
pricy handbag because she is
black
ask many a high-profile v.i.p stopped and searched
everywhere for being of
colour and off colour
because the masters of the free world are afraid of losing
their land to these invaders from
Africa
because these descendants of slaves just do not belong here
because because because
black is just neither normal nor human!

politics

they symbolise democracy
they define democracy
they decide the dividends of democracy
some say they are crazy.

politicians are proud of their profession
but critics ask them to make a confession
regarding the truth and lies
of a profession couched in lies.

questions follow questions
answers jam questions on the rebound
but answers are lost in the haze of questions that abound
on obsession with power and shady concessions.

what is democracy
who should define democracy
where to establish democracy
how to implement democracy?

democracy was imported by the revered masters from Britannia
they emphasise political parties and elections and the vote based upon the principles of freedom and majority victory and right to choose
they stress the duty of the executive and the legislature to enact laws and to uphold the constitution and to govern with the oversight of the judiciary playing the role of neutral and objective arbiter in a potentially explosive situation.

our politicians have learned the tenets and lessons of democracy
upside down according to the logic of the illogical
as one places the cart before the horse
as one reads a book upside down
as one consumes raw meat in the guise of the well-cooked offering.

they conceive of nation as an absolute creation of the almighty colonisers
untouchable unchangeable now and forevermore
not as a process of birthing and building unity
not as a concept encouraging various nationalities to sacrifice for the common good
not as generosity and selflessness
they forget that the notion of nation lies in the depths of independence and the collective soul
like the fiery fire of freedom burning bright and beautiful in the hearts of a committed community
they discountenance the basic desire to live and die together as one
they remain passionate only for their pockets
they remain eternal only in their contempt for the people
they patriotically replace the age of innocence
with the age of insolence.

they owe their education to the once rulers of the plantation named nation
the military and their incursion into politics
when dictatorship redefined democracy
 according to the rules of autocracy
when the tendency to decree and dictate
nullified any attempt to discuss and decide
after even-handed and well considered deliberations.

the military education has obliterated the line between
election and selection
the politician may be an ex-military man or a military
collaborator or acolyte
as they both act out their patriotism in the corridors of
stolen power
as they continue to compete for national booty
in the spring or summer of our discontent
as they remain tethered to tyranny
trend-setters that they are for an admiring public
willingly serving as sentinels for the patricides
as surrogates mouthing their gospel of patriotism
to a silent majority all too prepared for oppression by their
very lack of preparation.

our politicians are quick to invoke American democracy as
model
they travel to the land of the free and the home of the brave
to learn from their congress deemed the best and the
brightest on the globe
they spend one day at the capitol and one month in the hotel
and on the streets
seeking the dividends of civilisation in the most concrete of
terms
solid skin and greenbacks
mansions and myriad material means
they out-Americanise Americans
scandal fraud grand larceny murder and more in the name of
democracy
such are the lessons taken back from there to here
they forget the simple arithmetic of accountability
they insist that they are the owners of democracy
that they can use as they wish
they affirm that every blessed day belongs to patriotic

criminals
without exception
because they are both judge and jury
both defender and prosecutor
villain become hero
revered like the reverend.

our politicians believe in the party system and the electoral process
one man one vote
they know all about campaigning among the patriotic public
they recognise the sanctity of the freedom to choose
they therefore use their right and freedom
to rig
to bribe
to defraud
to stuff ballot boxes
to snatch victory from the grasp of true winners
deemed unworthy to represent the people
they engage in horse-trading and secret deals and blatant illegality
to prove their patriotism
in a land that they must protect and pillage and control in chaos
they rebuff all opposition as unpatriotic
they trade conscience for contaminated coins
they posit and pursue programmes perilous to the well-being of the people
they hype process to the detriment of product
they see the precipice staring them in the face
yet they do not relent in their headlong rush towards what they call paradise
they proudly pronounce the excellence of their stellar performance

perched upon the podium of shallowness and showmanship
in a context of conflict and confusion and callous
competition.

our politicians savour the right to jumbo remuneration
for work undone or badly done
for supposedly building sacred structures with stolen fortune
for purchasing mansions and castles abroad with public
funds
for destroying any and every semblance of development
while the impoverished populace keeps praying and praying
and praying
for the armed robbers.

our politicians make heresy out of honourable acts of
patriotism
just as they would have us believe that America and Africa
share
the common bond of democracy
just as they tell the people that the slum shacks are
skyscrapers
just as they see no wrong in the people rummaging for food
in dung-heaps
just as they claim that mortuaries are maternity wards.

perhaps one should remind the prostituting patriots
of the words of an American son true to the tenets of
democracy
words that our pimping patriots might use as driving force
for their tainted souls:
ask not what your country can do for you
ask what you can do for your country!

ode to Africa's dinosaurs

The doctrines of democracy deal with the aspirations of men's souls, but the application deals with things. (Zora Neale Hurston)
you seized power by the gun-barrel or the gimmicky ballot
you
promised to lead the people to paradise
and they praised
you
and you promised them
heaven on earth
not hell not hate not hype.

you
messiah of the masses
you
prince of progress and peace and prosperity
you
saviour of society
you
supreme guide of God's sheep on earth.
(REPARATIONS ARE BEING SOUGHT FROM THE WEST
FOR CENTURIES OF SLAVERY AND COLONIALISM)

you
quickly sold your soul to the west and turned your country
into a wasteland
human carnage carrion corpses carcasses galore
were soon scattered all over the battlefields of our land
you

began to maim and mangle men and minds
you
monstrous murderous messiah
you
cynical son of satan
you
supreme commander of our killing fields.

you
promised to build not to destroy
dreams of a better tomorrow
yet our tomorrow is today
like yesterday in hell
you
condemned past leaders
for their graft greed mindless materialism
yet your doctrine of death defies definition
as you ride in your armoured limos and hide in your fortified mansion
constructed with our people's blood and bones.
(A NATIONAL ONE-WEEK HOLIDAY IS DECLARED IN HONOUR OF MR. PRESIDENT'S BIRTHDAY AND HIS FIRST LADY'S RETURN FROM VACATION)

you
love the people like a plague
you
let them live by lynching them
by providing them with nothing
by urging them to suffer in silence like good children of God
you
exude generosity with your bulging personal bank account
by giving away the people's money to the filthy rich and your innumerable bed daughters

you
practise your godliness like the devil
and
the people love
you
to
death.
(A NATIONAL DAY OF CELEBRATION IS DECLARED IN HONOUR OF MR. LIFE-PRESIDENT'S ASSASSINATION TODAY)

you
supreme guide
saviour
prince
messiah
you
cannot save yourself
when the people pounce upon
you.

your ears They will
cut
because you refused to
listen
your eyes They will
gorge out
because you refused to
see
your legs They will
break
because you led Them to hell
because you walked all over Them
your brain They will

snuff out
because you refused to
think of Them
your head They will bring down
because you refused to be
symbol of success and sacrifice and sanity and sanctity for
Them
because
because
because you refused to be
one with
Them!

love and pain

tears unseen long construed as symbol of self-control and hardiness
tears finally flow on a sad day of shock
remember the short note announcing man's mortality
remember everyone's frozen frame of body and mind
upon learning that their old man was human
after all those years of believing in the magic of cool
remember the one drop that made my little girl cry and crumble
as her siblings look askance at the debunking of a myth
and the restoration of basic humanity.

those tears should have confirmed the love we've always had
misunderstood by most
misinterpreted by self-appointed analysts
mistaken for lack of love by detractors
unseen by those with eyes blinded by bias
unappreciated by those incapable of feeling without showing and telling.

a heart given is a treasure of unfathomable value
unlike material and its many imitations and limitations
you give your heart but it may be taken away from the taker.

one day you're soaring in the skies
feeling like superman in a perfect world
the next day there you are suddenly dipping
dipping
dipping towards disaster

as if feeling good were never in your sign and system
as if you were condemned from birth
to suffer pain
to roll and reel in pain
pain without respite
pain with no relief
pain without rest
yes, maybe tomorrow
tomorrow
tomorrow that will surely come
tomorrow that may never come
in life or death
while pain remains a constant
even in love.

this came ages ago expressing hopes on love:
together
we can find happiness in spite of all the barriers
both deep and superficial
together
we can laugh and love
we can even be sad in times of sorrow
together
knowing that we are sharing
together
your love of music and dance
of nature and good food
they are not different from mine if only I take the time
together
we must find that time
to love
in spite of the pain
ever present it is
and pain knows no boundaries

just like love
and pain knows no love
and pain knows
no pain but pain.

one life fulfilled
(for Nelson Mandela, Robben Island Prisoner #46664)

Breaking News: Nelson Rolihlahla Mandela, icon of the struggle for freedom, conscience of the world, anti-apartheid leader and the first democratically elected president of South Africa, passed at age 95 on December 5, 2013.

a comet of unknown departure and destination crashes into the strange sea of a place called Aiye
the ancestral baobab comes uprooted as thunder and lightning bolts shake the earth battered by rains cast in a rainbow of colours
daylight turns into midnight and humans and mammals and all elements of nature are yet to understand these phenomena in their despair at the southern colossus that has shocked the universe by taking his final breath expected but dreaded
the whole world remains in shock
we are witnessing the spontaneous adulation of universal flock
with condolences of love and reverence pouring in from all sides
Madiba is dead
Mandela is gone
leaving an irreplaceable hole in the global heart.

a crossroads of tears and laughter marks the departure of a life fulfilled
and, remarkably, laughter trumps tears because Madiba's life signifies joy
friends and foes alike admire him

Femi Ojo-Ade

man and nature stop to salute him
the legendary troublemaker that shakes the traditional tree
the famous boxer learning the art of aggression for a strategy of defence
the stick-fighter using the capoeira tactics to create a bastion of attack and counter-attack against the formidable foe of his people
he was born into royalty on the Qudu hills where he learned the nitty-gritty of culture including the force of consensus and the wisdom of the elders
his youthful zeal for freedom coupled with his love of life and devotion to the destitute and valuation of the commoners in his society of privileges
he became a lawyer and an activist combining aggression with defence in the name of freedom and justice and human rights
Mandela the rebel against racist reaction and apartheid's separatist supremacism.

the man's mien and demeanour give away his uniqueness
tall as a totem pole
straight as a ramrod
unwavering as a skyscraper in the southern skies
the strapping figure of a potentially harmful giant soon reveals his gentility and desire to help and not harm
his infectious smile breaks now and then into an angelic reassuring laughter
the laughter disarms his avowed enemies dislodged from their perch of prejudice and paternalism
the laughter invites and welcomes his friends and family into a cocoon of confidence and comfort and a haven of harmony and happiness
yet the seemingly facile construct of solidity and solidarity is a creation of complexity and controversy

a tale of miracles with death leading to life.

Rivonia was supposed to mark the end
Mandela the terrorist was condemned to life in prison
he defied the apartheid terror and all the odds
he vowed to live to fight or to die fighting
Robben Island was the chosen space of torture and isolation
of assault on human dignity and absolute dehumanisation
 the prisoner saw mainland so near but so far away
he saw the ocean serving as symbol of the impossibility of
reconnection to roots and to the reality of true living daring
him to dream
the prisoner rejected dream as he envisioned reality and
revival
he was forced to break stones as an act of engagement in
nothingness and
proof of the dead end to which he and his comrades were
condemned
the very presence of comrades defeated apartheid's
monstrous machine of murder
Robben was changed into a collective of the committed
microcosmic of the anti-apartheid movement
debates and exchanges and analyses and assessments honed
the skills and prepared the content of character of our one
and only president.

Madiba underwent twenty-seven years of education in
courses as diverse as
history and humility
freedom and forgiveness
justice and injustice
human rights and responsibilities
respect and reconciliation
when he strolled majestically out of the shadow into the

sunshine on that fateful day in 1990
he was ready to rule
not as a dictator but as a democrat immersed and versed in consensus
not as a hate-filled black racist but as a humble human being with deep understanding of foibles and frailties
he came to lead a united rainbow nation
not a black island
he came to establish and promote peace
not to propagate a war of revenge and retribution
he came to show the unique qualities of the human spirit
not to propel a machine of hate hounding down an enemy misled by his ignorance and pomposity
that is why he compelled his people to throw away their pistols and panga and embrace peace.

Madiba is an African
a man of integrity
an intrepid spirit fighting for freedom
a soul rooted in the depths of Africa's soil
trustworthy and timeless
respected and respectable
African to the core in terms of history and heritage
steeped in the pride of purpose of a great civilisation
his aura and charm and genius
made for global successes such as the world cup hosted for the first time in Africa
in spite of his open relationship with perceived pariahs to the capitalist hegemonies.

Madiba they say is a communist
commie murderer
commie terrorist
commie marxist

commie racist
so rail many a right-wing reactionary
communist because he is fighting for his people's freedom and rights
communist when he reaffirms faith and solidarity with fellow fighters for human rights
communist because he insists on standing by those that stood by him in times of need
communist when he stands up against oppression and repression and hate and hypocrisy.

almighty America stood out among mandelaphobists in tandem with the Queen's dilapidated empire
they concocted the strange language of constructive engagement with a renegade regime engaged in destroying everyone and everything black
the iron lady and her American steely collaborator led an army propping up the supremacists' economy and restraining freedom with chains and shackling justice
they cooperated with the apartheid monster in peddling the joys of poverty and pandering to pompous propaganda
until Mandela mesmerised them with his victory over threats of coup and chaos
in a free and fair election heralding true democracy in a land once despotic under the caprices of dictators.

here we are in Soweto stadium on a rainy day in December
to honour the memory of our departed Tata
to celebrate the life of our dear Khudu
all are present for Mandela
capitalists and communists
left and right
good and bad
they are redefined and refined into a diverse humanity

politics is placed on the backburner
and humanity takes centre-stage for a change.

the motley crowd is star-struck
not by the very important personalities alighting from their sleek limos
but by the ever increasing shadow of our departed Father
the uniqueness of this singular star is that he has aroused the commoners' self-worth and pride and identity as full-fledged human beings
Madiba makes you proud
Madiba makes you confident
Madiba makes you you
a man
a woman
an African.

Soweto
is a vivid symbol of our struggle
it's the site of apartheid torture and massacre
it's the hotbed of white-hot hate where children were mowed down by goons wielding guns
it's the home of Bantu Biko and his fellow martyrs teaching us never to forget
it's the venue where Madiba's daughter read his response rejecting the monster's offer of pseudo-freedom in exchange for his soul to be silenced in a peace of the cemetery
it's also the venue of that rugby match in which Madiba dexterously aroused in many prejudiced minds love of the other in the rainbow nation by donning the apartheid-drenched jersey bearing the captain's number
Soweto stands as symbol of the new nation.

the people are there singing and dancing

in celebration of a life fulfilled and in honour of their hero
and father and grandfather
they are daring the rain and other elements of nature as
proof of their courage and commitment
they know that rain is a blessing by the deities bringing
peace and calm to the earth and to human hearts
they keep coming and coming and coming
in the communal spirit of Ubuntu
underscoring kindness and interconnectedness and
forgiveness:
I am because you are.

the speeches all reflect Madiba's extraordinary global
influence and his status as a giant towering over minnows
and a rarified light in a world of darkness
Ban-Ki Moon mentions Mandela's anger at injustice, not at
individuals
Obama thanks South Africans for sharing the last great
liberator of the twentieth century with the world and for
celebrating a life like none
he reminds us of Mandela's words emphasising the man's
humanity:
*I'm not a saint except you think of a saint as a sinner who
kept trying.*

Madiba's married life might be placed under the microscope
of dissection and destruction by detractors always ready to
sneer at black accomplishments
to the stigma of communist would be added the reputation
of a lothario running after any moving being in skirts
the dignity accorded the women in his life on this special day
debunks any ill repute
Madiba's widows are both recognised and duly respected at
the Soweto ceremony

Winnie's case is the source of controversy
but it is also an example of human consideration
because it highlights the couple's sacrifice for the cause of the nation
Madiba divorced Winnie but never abandoned her
he acknowledged that she had it more difficult than he
given her torture in the hands of the apartheid regime
and her exposure as a woman to unscripted moments of harassment and humiliation
if the end of the Winnie chapter made Madiba the loneliest man in the world
Graça came as a return to the sunshine of life and love
and the two women sit there mourning together their great loss
they embrace each other solemnly in sincere empathy of a shared loss of one love
and their faces frowning with pain are fixated on a distance where their departed man
is breaking into that seductive smile declaring that everything is all right
and they both smile, subtly, accepting fate and resting assured that all will be well.

the capitalists' notorious commie stood head and shoulders above all the controversies swelling around him
he won over one and all
he separated politics from personal programmes and projections
even as he combined political savvy with human sensitivities
which is why a hundred thousand of the mass of the people
congregated with a hundred masters of the globe in Soweto
when the conscience of the world breathes his last
Nelson Mandela, there is no one like you!

yet it is cogent to ask about the destitute of Soweto and Alexandra
since we know that Madiba's principles and programmes included the eradication of poverty and the realisation of equality and justice and human rights in his rainbow society
Madiba's presidency never must we forget
laid the foundation for the future
it was the beginning not the end
 his revolution born out of reaction and retrogression would lead to peaceful evolution
his point of departure was to lead to his people's point of arrival
no surprise that revolution brought peace but not prosperity for Blacks
Madiba brought political freedom but not financial fortune for Blacks
he laid the groundwork for development
for Blacks
in a land where Whites remain in control of the economy
where Whites hoarded the beautiful space in the cities and beyond
where Blacks were condemned to slum townships like Alexandra and Soweto
where their right of presence and identity as humans was attached to a pass
where the disgusting document was annulled by Mandela's triumph
awakening hope in the downtrodden and making Soweto and all symbol of the new nation.

yet symbolic nullification did not for status elevation make
townships are what they used to be
the eyesore of a nation reeking of powerlessness and poverty
in stinking waterless no-amenities shacks years after

Madiba's honourable step-down
although the pass was shredded as entry visa to white
paradise of plenty
the act did not dent the dehumanising conquest of white
Power shamelessly pummeling black Poverty perennially
kept in their place
Sowetoans are now free to visit Jo'burg and Sandton without
a pass
even if only to window shop or to gawk at the rich on display
and in play
even if just to offer their service for a fee as butler or cook or
whatever as they used to be
even if only to serve as nannies fawning upon white children
while theirs are left at home or privileged to come with them
to envy the boss's child or dream impossible dreams
Blacks are frozen in stasis
like have-nots in a steal-all society
like oppressed poor condemned to the back of the social bus
like the mass being pissed upon in the valley by the masters
perched upon the mountain.

Yet we remember that some Blacks live in white heaven on
earth
black bourgeois beneficiaries of Mandela's magnificence and
magnanimity have failed to fulfill his promise of plenty for
the poor people
their upward mobility is concretised in corruption and
colour-blindness and conscience-blankness
hardly is any fit enough to shine Madiba's shoes
they latch on to the Struggle like desperate cowards
drowning but afraid to die
and ready to die in order to maintain a status stolen through
reputation and not honest work
they are in power and must remain in power because they

belong to the clan of the committed
they forget that commitment can be viable only if anchored
in a community in the name of whom the Struggle was
begun and ended
they remember only the spoils cornered by them at the top
they remember the people only at election time
they forget that the people will remember
some day soon.

all should remember Madiba's words:
to overcome poverty is not an act of charity but a gesture of justice.
also says he:
I gave dignity to the white man.
words of wisdom and conciliation they are
a challenge to Black and White to come together on behalf of
the people
words of challenge that forged reconciliation but not change
because Whites remain racist and rich swimming in gold
and Blacks — the leaders — have become selfish and
irresponsible
yet they were once responsible and responsive to cooperation
with others
to advance the cause of the Struggle through divestment and
sanctions
with brothers and sisters and friends from afar in Europe and
America
such as the Black Caucus in American congress and other
individuals
and Africa was not left behind with Nigeria leading the way
with billions of dollars
in a United Nations lobby that led to the creation of a special
committee leading to sanctions against the barbaric regime
Nyerere of Tanzania was right there on the frontline with his

country hosting ANC's headquarters
yet Nigeria's current president is reduced to silence on a back
seat at Madiba's memorial
because his giant of a country has become a gnome in many
an arena of responsibility
most notably on that fateful day when arguably its most
terrible tyrant ordered the summary execution of human
rights activist Saro-Wiwa
while its three foremost writers joined world leaders and
Madiba in seeking a reprieve and a review of the death
sentence passed by a court of the corrupt working towards
the answer and arriving at a decision before a discussion
Nigeria has lacked focus and savvy
so much so that it has reaped contempt for her commitment
that has transmuted into a long season of corruption
Madiba never forgot that impunity and that act of barbarity
while some steeped in imperialistic greed returned to
business as usual with a country long on potential but short
on performance.

Zimbabwe also fell from grace to grass in the person of a
leader once the icon of guerrilla warfare and hero of the
people's struggle through which the apartheid-like regime
was sent back to Britain
he loves power so much that he has become a life president
misbehaving in the vein of a nonentity dipped in criminality
and ready to kill and not be killed as long as he remains
perched on his terrible throne
he stands with one leg on the edge of the grave and may be
buried standing on the other
Africa's leaders are largely a shame in spite of Madiba.

some of the prominent world leaders showering praise on
Madiba

hide their badge of shame under the hypocritical coat of honour
history — of which they are the makers — allows them to wallow in amnesia
that we the victims will never allow
thus we remember that America's CIA tipped off apartheid's secret service to the arrest of
Madiba and his twenty-seven-year sentence at Rivonia
we remember that America and Britain were staunch allies of apartheid
they were all partners in the progressive project of keeping Blacks under the latter's separatist sole
Britain's iron lady and America's hero of reaction called reaganomics used the ruse of constructive engagement to keep apartheid afloat in terrorist triumph
Mandela was on the American list of terrorists until 2008.

A message to Madiba:
As you join our ancestors in the final home not removed from here and us
Please remember our people, please
You sowed the seeds of hope
While your enemies spread hatred
You taught us that life is sacred
That on the darkest days we can still cope and hope
If we remain true to our humanity and heritage and maintain our dignity.

You led us to the gates of the promised land
That some are trying to snap shut in our faces
Some deny your promise by their heinous acts
Others say the land of promise is already real and absolute
Both liars have their hardly hidden agenda of self-aggrandisement and desire to control

Egregious and everlasting corruption overpowering a people born and bred in humility and integrity.

Some ask questions about the promise and the land and the vision and the future
Cogent questions, one may admit, but there are answers right there in your life story
Informing us that ours is a destiny far better than our history of genocide in the hands of goons at home and abroad
That we can triumph only if we try with conviction through genuine commitment
Under a leadership willing to reject the lure of lucre and lead a life of true patriotism
In front of a people that they love
Without lying to them
Without luring them to sleep with false promises
Without lynching them.

Madiba, now our beloved ancestor
Tata, our loving father
Khudu, our revered grandfather
Mandela, our leader
Lala Ngoxilo, Hamba Kahle!
Rest in peace, Go well!

God save us

God
save
us
from
our despicable dictators
our lying and lustful leaders
our corrupt conveners of midnight meetings to share the national cake.

If
God
don't
save
us
from the endemic darkness imprisoning the city of lights
from the stench of a civilisation once deemed excellent
from the corruption of a land of integrity
from the poverty of a land blessed with immense wealth
wallowing in misery
if
God
don't
save
us
from man-made earthquakes-hurricanes-tsunamis-typhoons
in a country exempted by nature from such catastrophes
from those that steal from the poor to make themselves zillionaires
from those that devastate the land and transform it into a